Chaucer and the Medieval Book

Chaucer
and the Medieval Book

BY BEVERLY BOYD

THE HUNTINGTON LIBRARY
1973

Copyright © 1973
Henry E. Huntington Library and Art Gallery
Library of Congress Catalog Card Number 73-77021
Printed in the United States of America
by Anderson, Ritchie & Simon
designed by Ward Ritchie

To my parents

Contents

1. OF "bookes, clad in blak or reed"/3

2. PICTURES AND DECORATION IN BOOKS/28

3. WRITING IN BOOKS/58

4. BOOK TRADE AND LIBRARIES/89

5. CHAUCER, PUBLISHED AND PRINTED/113

APPENDIX/141

BIBLIOGRAPHY/159

INDEX/163

Illustrations

I Medieval English coins/10-11
Courtesy the Trustees of the British Museum, London

II Medieval manuscript containing two of the *Canterbury Tales*/20

III Blind-stamped binding (*ca.* 1515)/23
Courtesy the Bodleian Library, Oxford

IV Page from late thirteenth-century manuscript/34-35
Courtesy the Pierpont Morgan Library, New York

V Portrait of Chaucer, Ellesmere Manuscript/42

VI Portrait of Chaucer, early fifteenth century/45
Courtesy the Master and the Fellows of Corpus Christi College, Cambridge

VII Page from the Ellesmere Manuscript/68-69

VIII Secretary bookhand, fifteenth century/70-71
Courtesy the Bodleian Library

IX Page from the Campsall Manuscript/72-73
Courtesy the Pierpont Morgan Library, New York

X *Canterbury Tales*, Caxton's first edition (*ca.* 1478)/74-75

XI *Canterbury Tales*, Caxton's second edition (*ca.* 1484)/74-75

XII *Canterbury Tales*, illustration from Caxton's first edition/140
NOTE: *All illustrations not credited otherwise are from the Huntington Library*

Preface

CHAUCER is taught everywhere. It is not necessary to have a research library at hand in order to read and enjoy the works of this great poet of long ago. Chaucer studies on any advanced level, however, are another matter. Many graduate students have to function with very limited library facilities, and even in large universities instruction in essential background areas, including language, becomes a major problem as semesters grow shorter and as the demand increases for emphasis upon literary criticism. Under these circumstances bibliographical study can seldom receive serious attention in courses devoted to the poet and his works, even though it is sure to present itself to anyone who expects to deal with Chaucer—and indeed with Middle English literature—beyond the most elementary level.

This book is an introduction to those aspects of Chaucer studies which involve manuscripts and incunabula. Its purpose is not to discuss particular technical problems in Chaucer research, but to give the reader sufficient background information, and sufficient critical apparatus, so that he can not only work into these areas on his own if necessary, but read intelligently the major research in one of the most difficult branches of Chaucer study. Portability has also been an objective, so that the instructor who wishes to do so can use the book in connection with his courses. Hopefully, he will also persuade his students to take courses in related fields.

The reader need bring with him to the present study only an ability to read Middle English in Chaucer's dialect, and a general knowledge of Chaucer's times and afterwards, to 1500, which year marks the end of the earliest phase of printing. Unlike most studies of medieval books, this one considers the earliest work of the printing press an extension of the work of the scriptorium. There is in fact no radical difference between manuscripts and incunabula other than process, and, while typography is a field for specialists, no one should leave his training without knowing how to read a Caxton, and how to deal with the research on the earliest books printed in English.

In following these chapters the reader will need to know in advance how certain kinds of materials are ordered. In quotations from Middle English, u and v are written as in Modern English. Marks of punctuation are those used in Modern English. Scribal abbreviations have been expanded and underlined. Quotations from other languages have been translated, except in special cases as noted. References to the *Canterbury Tales* are cited by fragment and line. Quotations from Chaucer's works are from F. N. Robinson's second edition (Boston, 1957). The plates containing text have all been transcribed, whether or not the text is the reason for their inclusion. The transcriptions are all literal, rather than normalized, so that the reader may see what the text actually says, but scribal abbreviations, including symbols for *and*, are expanded and italicized. With regard to statistics and other data, the references are to the works where they are discussed, since these commentaries contain other pertinent information. While the subject of editing after 1500 is outside the scope of this volume, and therefore cannot be examined as a topic, editorial problems and practices are treated as they arise in the discussions.

The research that goes into so widely based a study as this necessarily acquires in the process debts that can never be acknowledged. My gratitude to the institutions that have granted me the means with which to work can hardly find suitable expression: to the American Council of Learned Societies, for a grant in the summer of 1968; to the University of Kansas, for grants in 1970 and in 1971; and to the John Simon Guggenheim Foundation, which made it possible for me to spend an entire academic year, 1969-70, in libraries in London, New York, and San Marino, Cali-

Preface

fornia. I hope the objectives of this book will justify their support.

For advice which cost them time and patience, I am indebted to the following of my colleagues of the University of Kansas: Thomas Weiss, Department of Economics; and Alexandra Mason and Ann Hyde, Department of Special Collections. I am also indebted for advice in matters pertaining to art history to Wendy Shadwell, New York City, and to Adelaide Bennett, Princeton, New Jersey. If these chapters prove less than worthy, the fault is certainly not theirs.

My investigations have taken me to many libraries, and I have received replies to numerous inquiries from staff members which it would be impossible to acknowledge properly. I am particularly grateful to Marion M. Archibald, Department of Coins and Medals, the British Museum, for several conferences regarding English coins, and for obtaining photographs; to A. R. B. Fuller, St. Paul's Cathedral Library, for making manuscript materials available to me; and to Curt F. Bühler, the Pierpont Morgan Library, New York City, as well as to the Director and other members of the staff, for the same; and to T. Kaye, of Trinity College Library, Cambridge, for investigating problems in manuscript references. I am particularly grateful to the Director, the Librarian, and the staff of the Henry E. Huntington Library, who had an entire year of my project and its problems.

Finally, to my parents, who suffered through the last stages of this writing, grateful thanks.

January, 1972

1
Of "bookes, clad in blak or reed"

No one can study Chaucer's poetry without recognizing that he was a man who loved books. Throughout his writings, he alludes to his own library, and to his absorption in reading. Precisely which books Chaucer may have owned one can only guess, for he has left no list. But much is known about the books available during his time, their appearance and structure, and the manner in which they were housed both for preservation and for use. Anyone who wishes to work with Chaucer's writings in their earliest extant form, and in fact with any late medieval texts, must learn to deal with books of the period in all their physical aspects.

The discussion which follows will be concerned not only with the fourteenth century, in which Chaucer lived and wrote, but also with the fifteenth, for it was that century which saw the production of the manuscripts in which his works have survived, as well as the production of the earliest printed editions.

It is appropriate to begin with bindings. Chaucer himself raises the topic in his portrait of the Clerk of Oxford:

> For hym was levere have at his beddes heed
> Twenty bookes, clad in blak or reed,
> Of Aristotle and his philosophie,
> Than robes riche, or fithele, or gay sautrie.
> ("General Prologue," I, 293-96)

Of the Clerk's twenty Aristotles as possessions of a threadbare scholar, there will be more to say later.[1] But the topic of medieval bookbinding as such has a significance of its own for Chaucer scholars, and not merely because bound books were part of the poet's milieu, although that is necessarily the case. More importantly, those manuscripts and printed copies of his works which have survived so many centuries owe their longevity not only to luck, but in large part to the skill of the craftsmen who first sewed them to their bands and attached them to the materials which protected them. To study these books, and to read the technical works that have been written about them, it is necessary to know how materials were prepared for binding.

This, unfortunately, does not mean that the Chaucer manuscripts present themselves as a treasure trove of the medieval binder's art. None of them, in the first place, is contemporary with the poet, and few survive in their original bindings. Time is not entirely to blame for this situation since medieval binding leathers have held up better, relatively speaking, than those of the nineteenth century.[2] But unless later collectors found them richly decorated and remarkably preserved, they had little interest in these relics of the past, preferring to have their valuable acquisitions rebound. The old bindings were then discarded, to the great loss of present-day research.

There are other problems. Books were not necessarily finished with permanent covers after they were sewn, and, since they were sometimes given new covers when they changed hands even among contemporaries, the covers are often later than the books they contain. An outstanding example of this is the library of Federico da Montefeltro, at Urbino, in the late fifteenth century. Described by the famous contemporary expert on books, Vespasiano da Bisticci, as the ideal library, its contents were uniformly bound in crimson and silver, with silver clasps, the Bible, bound in gold brocade, being the sole exception.[3] Bibliophiles of the time were in fact accustomed to have all their books uniformly bound. With regard to more common bindings, certain types made in the sixteenth century looked much the same as those made in the fifteenth century or even in the fourteenth. For all these reasons, it is useless to attempt a catalog of Chaucer manuscripts in bindings earlier than 1500, the terminal date of this study.[4]

✥ Of "bookes, clad in blak or reed"

As for Chaucer's personal books, there is no way of knowing how they were bound, and the present essay will concern itself, not with speculation in that area, but with ordinary books of the time, our interest being not with what he owned but with what he encountered at every turn and with what was familiar in the fifteenth century. The discussion assumes that most readers have seen volumes, or pictures of volumes, bound in boards and luxuriously decorated with jewels and precious metal, but that they are not so well acquainted with the appearance of more commonplace books. With this in mind, illustrations have been chosen from the Chaucer manuscripts to represent ordinary bindings characteristic of the late Middle Ages, without regard for precise date.

The subject of bookbinding has two principal aspects: a sewing operation and a process by which the sewn book is attached to covers. The second process may be followed by embellishment of the covers. This kind of art, however, must be understood in terms of the other two processes, for the general shape of a book is a product of custom. The book, as it has been known since the rise of Christianity, is the codex, or flat book, which replaced the scroll of the Graeco-Roman world. Since the subject of binding presumes gatherings to be bound to form a codex book, it is necessary to begin the discussion with the gatherings and their materials.

Writing material prepared from animal skin is known under the names "parchment" and "vellum." These terms are ambiguous. The *OED* describes vellum as a fine kind of parchment prepared from the skins of calves, lambs, or kids; also any superior kind of parchment,[5] whereas a fifteenth-century manuscript of Trinity College, Cambridge (MS. R. 14. 45, fol. 57 [p. 101]) gives directions for preparation which plainly indicate that the author understood parchment as sheepskin, vellum as calf. The only difference shown in the preparation is that calf is scraped on both sides:

Forto make Parchemyne
Forto make parchemyne gode and ffyne: Take the a schepis skynne

and caste hit inne lyme and water and late hit ligge ix dayes ther inne; thanne take hit up and streyne hit a brode on a harowe [hoop-shaped stretching device] made for the nonys; thanne take suche a fleyssyng knyf as this parchemyners use and chaufe a wey the flesshe on the flesshe side and evermore loke that thou have pouder of chalk inne thi handys forto casten on the skyn so that hit mowe alle wey rennen a doune be forne the knyfe; than set houte thyn skynne on the harowe forto drye; thanne whanne hit is drye schave hit efte sonys on the flesche syde until hit be al smothe and thanne take thyn knyfe and kit hit of and rolle hit to geders.

To make Velyme
And if thou wille make velyme: Take the a kalves skynne and do ther with inne the same maner as thou dedist with thi schepis skynne, save for the her that is on the kalves skynne the nedis most schave hit on bothe sydys and a schepis skynne schal be shaven but on the flesshe syde, and alle wey loke that wolle of thin skynne be offe or hit come in the lyme.[6]

Unfortunately, those who produced books in the Middle Ages were in a better position than modern bibliographers to know what type of writing material went into their manuscripts. To identify now the specific animal source of membrane writing material, it would be necessary to have preserved in the course of preparation the papillary layer of the dermis, which contains gland and fat cells characteristic of the particular species. Membrane to be used for writing, however, is scraped beyond that, down to the reticular layer. The reticular layer contains collagen fibres, which form patterns to some extent characteristic of the animal species, but these are not sufficiently exact to permit scientifically accurate identification by their means alone.[7] Identification of the animal species therefore depends upon other factors, such as the size of the book, its provenience, and its nature. Vellum was, in general, more expensive than sheepskin parchment, could be had in larger sizes, and was more durable.[8] Nowadays, however, manufacturers of stationery have settled these words for the public by using the term "vellum" to denote a suede-like finish

Of "bookes, clad in blak or reed"

and "parchment" to denote a crisp finish. With regard to membrane writing material, various sources express a preference for one term rather than the other as a generic name, leaving the scholar not only with the dilemma of making his own choice and being consistent, but with an even more troublesome uncertainty about the precise meaning of these terms in the references he consults. In the present study, parchment will be the generic name for membrane writing material, unless another meaning is specified.

Parchment did not at once fall into disuse with the appearance of printing in the fifteenth century, but it was impractical for mass production. The forty-two line (Gutenberg) Bible, of which about thirty copies are thought to have been printed on vellum, required for each copy 170 calf skins, or, for all copies, the skins of more than 5,000 calves.[9] Paper was easier to obtain, easier to use since it folded more readily, and had other affinities to the processes involved in printing, since it held printers' ink better than parchment and it did not stretch or buckle irregularly when damp. Nor did paper make its first appearance in European books with the advent of printing, for some manuscripts had been written on paper and some contained both paper and parchment, parchment having the virtue of greater strength. The one very real objection to the use of paper for books was resistance on the part of the public. People feared that paper would be impermanent. Their fears were not then justified, as the present condition of Caxton's papers witnesses so many hundreds of years later, though this is not to say that all paper has done as well.

Because certain attributes of paper have importance in indicating how a book was produced, it is necessary to know how paper was made in Europe during the later Middle Ages. Paper had been introduced into Spain by the Moors during the twelfth century, although it had been invented much earlier in China.[10] In the later Middle Ages, European paper was made from fermented pulp, itself made from linen or linen rags. Sheets of paper were produced by a rigid mold, which was a frame covered with a wire screen. The papermaker dipped the mold into the pulp, then raised it to a horizontal position over the vat to drain while he shook it sharply back and forth and from side to side to distribute the pulp evenly and to make the fibres cross. He then slipped the resulting sheet of paper onto a sheet of absorbent felt, and the process was repeated until a stack of alternating felt and paper had accumulated. The stack was then put in a press to remove the water. After that, the sheets of paper were hung to dry, sized, and polished. The paper made by this process, called laid paper, bears translucent lines from contact with the paper mold. The heavy lines running across the width of the sheet, about an inch apart, are called chain lines. The fine lines, running the length of the paper, are called wire lines. There may also be a watermark, produced by a pattern in the screen, which was the papermaker's trademark.[11] This shows in the center of one half of the sheet. There was little change in the basic method by which paper was produced in Europe until the nineteenth century.

The average size of paper molds used in medieval Europe was about 14 by 19 inches. The largest known sheets of paper measured 18½ by 26½ inches. Caxton's largest paper was 15¾ by 22 inches, but he used this only for the first and second editions of the *Golden Legend*. For all his other books, including the Chaucers, he used smaller papers, varying in size from 11 by 16 inches to 13 by 18½ inches.[12] This paper was imported from the Continent, probably from Belgium. The first paper mill in England was set up in Hertfordshire near the end of the fifteenth century, by John Tate. His paper, watermarked with a star and two cartwheels, was used by Caxton's successor, Wynkyn de Worde.

It is necessary to know how writing material was sold and how much it cost. James E. Thorold Rogers, whose sources are accounts of Merton College, Oxford, finds parchment quoted at 1½*d*. and at 1*d*. per skin in 1319 and in 1324, and at 3*s*. per dozen in 1399, although these figures reveal nothing about quality and size, which would have influenced the price. He notes a purchase by the quire in 1379.[13] Paper was sold by the quire, as well as by the ream, though it is uncertain what precise count these terms, which now mean twenty-four sheets and twenty quires, respectively, denoted in the Middle Ages. Quire also meant booklet in

&§ *Of "bookes, clad in blak or reed"*

the sale of parchment, especially in the universities, and the term had a further application to a small book, as in the case of *The Kingis Quair* of James I of Scotland.[14] The Paston letters in 1469 refer to quires used for letter writing.[15]

Returning to the accounts of Merton College: they quote vellum at 1½d. per skin in 1301, and in 1308 at both 3s. 2d. and 6s. per dozen, the difference presumably being in size and quality. In 1326, Rogers finds it purchased at Bicester by the sextary, though it is not clear what sextary means when applied to writing material.[16] A cheaper way of obtaining parchment for writing was to salvage material already used, by washing or by rubbing down the surface with pumice.

With regard to paper, prices need not, for present purposes, be carried farther back than Caxton's time. William Blades compiled a list of prices from a contemporary cost book of the Florentine Ripoli Press (1474-83). Bearing in mind that Caxton had to import his paper, these prices are useful. Since they are Italian (of Tuscany), Blades worked out a table of currency values (1480):

Florin: gold; 53 gr. (less than half the value of the English rose noble, 119 gr. or 10 shillings); 6 *lire*, 2 *soldi*.
Lira:. 20 *soldi*
Soldo: 12 *denari*

The term *lira* and its French cognate *livre* (now *franc*) both derive from Latin *libra* 'pound.' In this money, prices per ream are as follows, with the qualification that they denote standards not necessarily identifiable now:[17]

	lire,	*soldi*
	(per ream)	
1. Large paper of Bologna in common folio	6	8
2. Middling (medium) paper of Bologna in common folio	3	10
3. Small paper of Bologna in common folio	3	0
4. Paper of Fabriano, with crossbow watermark	3	6
5. Paper of Fabriano, with cross watermark	2	6

a. EDWARD III. Noble. Mint of Calais (denoted by flag on obverse). 1369-77

b. EDWARD III. ½ Noble. Mint of London. 1346-51

c. EDWARD III. ¼ Noble. Mint of London. 1361-69

d. EDWARD III. Groat. Mint of London, Series B 1351

Of "bookes, clad in blak or reed"

e. EDWARD III. ½ Groat. Mint of London. 1361-69

f. EDWARD III. Penny. Mint of London. 1361-69

g. EDWARD III. ½ Groat. Mint of London. Series B 1351

h. EDWARD III. Farthing. 1361-69

i. EDWARD III. ½ Penny. 1361-69

PLATE I. English coins in use during Chaucer's lifetime

6. Paper of Colle	2	6
7. Paper of Prato	2	10
8. Paper of Pescia, with spectacles watermark	2	18
9. Paper of Pescia, with glove watermark	2	8

With the florin less than 5 English shillings of the time, 1 florin equal to 6 *lire* 2 *soldi*, the most expensive of these papers cost about a florin, 5 English shillings, per ream; the cheapest cost 2 *lire* 2 *soldi*, a third of this. Paper in the late fifteenth century was cheaper than it had been before, because rags, instead of natural flax or linen textile, were used in its manufacture.

Quires or gatherings for books are made up by various methods of folding and assembling the sheets. In the Middle Ages books were produced in folio, quarto, or octavo, chiefly in folio. In this usage, "folio" means that the gatherings were made from sheets folded once by bringing together the top and bottom edges. This produced a booklet of two leaves or four pages, into which other booklets, folded in the same manner, could be inserted. Of course, the same result could be achieved by placing together two or more sheets and folding them simultaneously, except that the sheets would, in that case, be harder to fold.

A typical English manuscript was produced in folio, the gatherings being composed of four sheets (eight leaves or sixteen pages). Such a gathering is called a "quaternio" or "quaternion." But scribes were often inconsistent about the number of sheets in their gatherings, even within the same manuscript. Scholars studying textual problems involving possible losses or insertions of leaves have to study the makeup of individual gatherings. It is therefore necessary to know that parchment gatherings were matched before they were written so that the skin sides of the leaves, and the hair sides, faced each other, accommodating the slight differences in the surfaces. The first leaf or folio had the hair side outward: that is, recto. A missing leaf would upset this matching, as probably would also an insertion, unless it was planned very skillfully.

Quarto books were produced from gatherings in which, after the sheet had been folded once, it was folded again, so that one

◆§ *Of "bookes, clad in blak or reed"*

fold was parallel to the longer side, and one to the shorter side, of the original sheet. This, too, could be augmented by inserting another quarto booklet (though not more) between the second and third leaves. Octavo books were made from gatherings having a third fold.

If a book is made of paper, the positions of the chain lines, and of the watermarks, if any, are useful evidence as to the manner in which the gatherings were prepared. A book produced in folio has its chain lines running vertically, parallel with the center fold. A watermark would appear in the middle of one leaf or folio when the sheet was folded. The other folio would, of course, have none. In quarto books, the chain lines are horizontal, and the watermark is in the middle of the second fold. In an octavo book, the chain lines are once again vertical, and the third fold incorporates the watermark in the top corner. The fact that there are not enough watermarks in a gathering, or that there are too many, indicates that a leaf has been lost or added. Manly and Rickert have found instances in manuscripts of the *Canterbury Tales* in which leaves have been removed or added by the original scribe, producing abnormal gatherings.[18]

Some manuscripts contain both parchment and paper—four manuscripts of the *Canterbury Tales* are mixed. Additional MS. 5140 (1470-1500) of the British Museum is an interesting example. A paper quaternion is placed between two parchment folios to form the gatherings, obviously for strength.[19] Books printed on paper in the same period may have narrow strips of parchment, applied with paste, for the same purpose of reinforcement. These are now called "slips."

The manuscripts of the *Canterbury Tales*, some of which contain other works by Chaucer and works by other authors, have an additional importance as a cross section of English vernacular books of the late Middle Ages. They are chiefly in folio, and mainly in quaternion, although other types of gatherings may be found, including gatherings made from a single sheet in folio. Those of paper (there are twenty-eight) usually have twenty or twenty-four leaves or folios per gathering. As for Caxton, he worked mainly in folio, although he also printed some of Chaucer's short poems in quarto editions which are more in the nature of pamphlets than of books.

Foliation (numbering) was done by placing a number in the top right margin, recto, folio meaning the entire leaf of the folded sheet. Scholars cite pages of manuscripts by the folio numbers, recto and verso, although it is usual to omit the citation "recto." Recto and verso may be cited as *r* and *v*, or as *a* and *b*, superscript. Thus, a reference to folio 89, recto, of a manuscript would appear as fol. 89 or f. 89; a reference to the same folio, verso, would appear as fol. 89^v, fol. 89^b, or as f. 89^v, f. 89^b. Inclusive foliation is cited in much the same manner as inclusive pagination: i.e., fols. 88-89^v, fols. 88-89^b; or ff. 88-89^v, ff. 88-89^b. Some scholars write foll. for the plural. In cases where references are to columns of the pages, scholars use the letters *a* and *b* for references to the columns, reserving *recto* and *verso* for the foliation, and spelling out these words in cases that might involve ambiguity or general lack of clarity.

Especially in printing, it was necessary to keep track of the sheets, so that, when collected and collated for binding, their sequence within the gatherings, and the sequence of the gatherings themselves, could be quickly and accurately recognized. This is still done, by means of alphabet codes with numbers, called signatures, placed in the bottom margin of each sheet. Although they were sometimes trimmed away in very early printed books during binding, the signatures, where they exist, are a more accurate reference tool than foliation, which was usually done after the book was sewn and therefore after any mistakes in assembling the gatherings had already been made. References to signatures are made by the alphabet and number code, recto and verso, usually noted as *r* and *v*: i.e., sig. a1, sig. a1^v. Since the signatures themselves appear only on the first half of a gathering, scholars using them for references must supply them thereafter. The system of signatures sounds more complicated than it is, the essential point being that the folded sheets bear only one signature, so that the binder, working with a book in quaternion, knew that he had all

Of "bookes, clad in blak or reed"

the sheets when he had accounted for sig. a1 through sig. a4. Printed books of the period under discussion which have lost their signatures through trimming (assuming that they had signatures to begin with), are sometimes foliated or even paginated. In such cases, scholars are obliged to use whatever type of enumeration is provided. Again, the letters *a* and *b* are used to designate columns.

The binding of the gatherings to form a book was not necessarily done on the premises where the rest of the work had been carried out, though manuscript books copied to order were probably bound as part of the contract. It should never be assumed that any binding is necessarily of the same provenience as the volume it contains, although, of course, it may be. This is especially true of printed books, which were shipped all over Europe packed in barrels, the gatherings just as they had left the printer's hands. While printers undoubtedly kept specimen copies of their work in bindings, which were either of their own making or done to their order and specification by someone else, it does not follow that every printer had a binder on his staff. Indeed, there is plenty of evidence that binders kept their own establishments, especially in university towns.

Since the binder often had no connection with the printer or copyist of his book, he had the responsibility of seeing that the gatherings were complete and in order before beginning any work of his own. He also had to see that any handwork, such as paragraph marks and initials, was supplied. In the scriptorium, this work was the province of a specialist, called a rubrisher or rubricator. Eventually, printers learned to do all these things mechanically, so that the binder's services became limited to the actual sewing and covering operation, which began when the gatherings had been ordered.

The bindings of medieval books consisted of four basic materials: thread, usually linen; thongs for lacing; boards; and covering material, which might be leather, parchment or vellum, velvet, or embroidered textile. The only really vital items were thread and thongs, by which the gatherings were put together, for all books were not necessarily laced into boards. Indeed, many books survive which have never been given permanent covers after sewing. Occasionally, heavy tanned leather was used in bookbinding instead of boards, and in the fifteenth century binders experimented with pasteboard for the purpose.

Assuming, however, that the handwritten or printed book was ready in ordered gatherings for the binding process, the binder would first stitch each gathering, not directly to its adjacent gatherings all the way down the spine, but to a series of thongs, sometimes split or doubled, or cords, intended eventually to be laced into boards and secured with pegs. These thongs or cords were attached vertically to a rectangular frame placed on a table.[20] To facilitate the sewing, the binder might first punch a series of holes through the fold in the center of each gathering. Then, holding each gathering against the thongs, he brought a needle with linen thread through the first hole, looped it around the thong next to the hole, then brought it back through the same hole and up the page to the next hole, where the process was repeated until the last hole had been reached and finished. When at least one more gathering had been added and completed, he made a loop, known as a kettle stitch, as the last stitch. This was also done on the return sewing, so that there was a kettle stitch at the top and bottom across the spine. When the process was completed, the thongs were in the form of bands, dangling at the ends, which could eventually be laced into boards. Not included in this process were the head and tail bands, which were made after the book had been put into boards.

The idea of lacing codex books into boards, and of covering the boards with leather, is thought to have been originally Coptic. The combination was used everywhere in Europe in the Middle Ages. In England, the boards used were oak almost exclusively, though other woods have been identified: lime, chestnut, and sycamore. The fact that oak was readily available no doubt suggested the choice, but this wood was known to be durable, as well as strong and heavy. Weight was very important, for parchment tends to buckle and pressure was needed to keep the pages of the manuscript flat and to keep it closed. Often the weight was not

Of "bookes, clad in blak or reed"

enough and straps or clasps were added. In preparing the boards for use, the corners which were to form the opening of the book were either smoothed out but left plain, or shaped with a chisel, the latter being more usual in Chaucer's time.[21]

More than one method could be used for lacing books to boards. The objective was to attach the book to the boards durably, flexibly, and neatly. The boards had to be prepared for lacing, and, since there was more than one method of doing this lacing, there were different types of precut apertures. In the twelfth century, some books were laced by pulling the bands through tunnels drilled through the edges of the boards, into grooves on the insides. Through these they were pulled taut and secured with pegs. By this method, the bands were flat across the spine of the book, instead of rounded into the ridges more familiar in hand-bound volumes.[22] These are the result of a more common method by which, instead of tunnels, grooves were cut on the outside of the boards, having at their ends holes leading to the insides of the boards. The bands were pulled over the spine, over the outsides of the boards through grooves and holes, and then pegged tightly on the inside. In either case, the pages were afterwards trimmed to fit the boards with a chisel or with a plane.

The next step, after the book was in its boards, was the addition of a lining piece and of the head and tail bands. The lining piece was intended to lie down the spine of the book, between the backs of the gatherings and the eventual covering. It could be a substantial piece of leather extending the full length of the spine, or else two pieces extending from the ends of the spine to the kettle stitch at top and bottom. In that case, the two pieces were sometimes attached to a third, thinner piece between them. Sometimes, too, the lining piece was extended at top and bottom to form the basis of tabs. The lining piece might itself be lined with a piece of attractive textile, especially if the book was to have tabs. There is an interesting binding of this description in the Huntington Library: HM 26052.

The headband and tailband were produced by sewing with threads, often in colors, over and under thongs, the sewing being attached to the kettle stitch at top and bottom of the spine. This produced not only a stout top and bottom anchor for the book in its boards, but an attractive finish still used in modern bookbinding, though the same effect can now be produced nonfunctionally with a tape simply pasted on. Once the sewing had been completed, the head and tail bands were laced into the boards and pegged.

The usual finish for a bound book in boards was leather. The problem of classifying medieval bookbinding leathers by animal species is not much different from that of distinguishing membrane writing materials. This is partly because skins for bookbinding were often not tanned but whittawed, a process no longer employed. The skin was cured in a bath of lime, alum, and salt, which produced an off-white color. Whittawed leather usually had a soft finish, though it could be hardened by paring and polishing. After whittawing, the skin could be further treated with a solution prepared from kermes, a red insect-parasite of the oak tree, analagous to cochineal. This produced a red or pink finish on the surface of the leather. Books covered with whittawed leather so treated may show only traces of color now, the rest having rubbed off, exposing the white below. The Clerk of Oxford's red Aristotles would probably have been bound with this kind of leather, so treated. Additional MS. 10340 of the British Museum (1400 and later), which contains *Boece*, "Truth," and the "General Prologue" to the *Canterbury Tales*, has a binding of this description, although it is not necessarily of the same date as the manuscript.[23]

There is little scientific information for identifying histologically the animal species of medieval bookbinding leathers, though the possibility of future investigation is not so reduced by paring and scraping as is the case with writing material. When any of the papillary layer of the dermis remains, the hair follicles can sometimes identify the species. Such scrutiny is not necessary in such obvious cases as pigskin and tanned calf, which can be recognized by their grain. But Graham Pollard shows instances in which whittawed leather has been assumed to be doeskin or deerskin,

Of "bookes, clad in blak or reed"

whereas histological examination has identified the leather as seal. He believes that bindings were made from almost any animal species available, including such unlikely candidates as rabbit and dog.[24]

A high percentage of books, however, with or without boards, were covered with vellum or parchment, which might be fitted to the book with flaps. HM 144 of the Huntington Library, a Chaucer manuscript, is covered in this manner, without boards. The bands are sewn on the outside through two pieces of blind-stamped leather (Plate II).[25]

The leather cover, carefully cut by a pattern for mitering and attached to boards, is now, however, the most familiar finish of medieval books. Pollard has identified three basic patterns, the objective being to achieve a neat diagonal join when the fore edge, top, and bottom were folded over the board. The earliest method, assuming that the edges of the leather had been cut off at the corners on the diagonal, was to sew the flaps together across the join. The next development was to make what Pollard calls a third miter: that is, to leave a strip of leather in the middle when cutting the material to accommodate the fold over the corner. The latest development was to have a third miter at the inner corners as well, next to the spine. Such a pattern made possible neat, durable corners.[26]

Obtaining an equally neat, durable finish at the head and tail of the spine was much more difficult. Simply trimming off the leather level with the edge of the volume would have left the raw edge exposed to damage at a place highly vulnerable to wear. A method often used, especially in the twelfth century, was, as already shown, to finish the spine with tabs produced from the lining piece and its own textile lining if any. In that case, the leather intended to form the ends of the spine was sewn onto the rest of the tab at the edges. Another method of dealing with the leather at the top and bottom of the spine, one used especially in the fifteenth century and not unlike that used now, was to double the leather back inside the spine. The headband could then be anchored to the end of the spine by sewing, producing a tight back. But the

PLATE II. A medieval manuscript containing two of the *Canterbury Tales*, bound in contemporary vellum, showing bands sewn on the outside

Of "bookes, clad in blak or reed"

method most commonly used in Chaucer's time was quite the reverse: doubling back the leather on the outside and sewing the headband through or over the outer leather of the spine. This method was usual after about 1250, but it is found on books much older.[27]

Not all medieval books have now, or had originally, devices for keeping them closed. The practice of installing a closing device cannot be precisely dated, but some books of about 1200 have them. The earliest device is a strap and pin, held closed by tension from the book itself but catches and clasps were typical closings in the fourteenth century. Since closing devices can be added at any time they are unreliable as evidence of the date or provenience of books. The addition of chains to books is not part of bookbinding and will be discussed later in connection with libraries.[28]

Medieval books begin with incipits, not with title pages. The title page evolved from various printers' experiments in the fifteenth century, being first used in a Chaucer book by Wynkyn de Worde (1498). Nor were titles customarily placed upon bindings, although some twelfth-century books with flat spines have them. MS. Phillipps 8136, a manuscript of the *Canterbury Tales* now in the Bodmer Library (Geneva), is bound in boards and in leather covers which have flaps of leather and red textile. Straps of the same red textile have been used to hold in place a nameplate under horn. Manly and Rickert think that the binding is original; if so, it is of about the same date as the manuscript, 1450-70, but this is open to question.[29] Bindings were for the most part left plain, though sometimes with the addition of corners and bosses to reduce wear. While jewels, ornamented metal, and enamelwork, such as cloisonné, might be added to bookbindings, this was not ordinarily done, and the techniques involved are proper to jewelsmithing, not to the art of bookbinding; thus they are not discussed here.

The particular method of decorating bound books which was done by the binders themselves, and which was the forerunner of many more recent methods of decorating books, was blind stamping. This technique required metal dies, similar to those used for striking coins. These dies, more commonly called stamps in this connection, had a design cut in intaglio: in this, the design is hollowed out rather than raised, as it is in relief. When the stamp was applied to moistened leather, the leather was forced into the cavity and the water was forced out, and the pattern afterwards appeared raised in relief upon the surface of the leather. For this technique, tanned leather was used, rather than whittawed, most commonly calf or pigskin.[30] The pattern in relief dried hard on tanned leather, and lasted well. A Chaucer manuscript with this kind of decoration on its bindings is MS. Selden Arch. B. 14 (1450-70) of the Bodleian Library (Plate III), a manuscript of the *Canterbury Tales*.[31]

Blind stamping, so called because color was not added in the process, is first seen in twelfth-century bindings. There are for some reason no known examples from the fourteenth century, although this in all likelihood means only that none has survived. The technique then reappears in fifteenth-century books. In the sixteenth century, binders favored panel stamping a central design onto their books, the rest of the design being supplied by rolls instead of by single stamps. In that century also, the discovery of gold-tooling techniques introduced more variety into bookbinding, which began to flourish as one of the important forms of art.

The earliest bindings done with blind stamping have been called "Romanesque," the later ones "Gothic."[32] The distinction is really unnecessary because there is little difference in the work produced except that the later binders had fewer stamps and hence fewer of them in their designs, probably because they were secular and had no institutional wealth behind them. The earlier binders, moreover, did not place uniform designs on the two covers. While certain stamps, and combinations of stamps, can be traced to particular binders, who are consequently known by such interesting sobriquets as "the Scales Binder" (London), "the Demon Binder" (Cambridge), and "the Unicorn Binder" (Cambridge), the identification of any design as characteristically English in this period is deceptive. The designs of the twelfth-century binders were representative of the new interest in ecclesiastical architec-

◆§ Of *"bookes, clad in blak or reed"*

PLATE III. Blind-stamped binding *ca.* 1515

ture and iconography that flourished throughout Europe. In the fifteenth century, the art of printing, and the arts of papermaking, woodcut making, and blind stamping, came to England with professionals who were either foreign or trained abroad, especially in the Low Countries. Their art can hardly be described as English. The printers who concern the present study, Caxton, Pynson, and Wynkyn de Worde, themselves fit this description, for both Pynson and de Worde were Continental-born and, presumably, trained, while Caxton himself learned to print and did his own earliest work abroad.

It should be remembered that a printer did not necessarily have anything to do with the binding of books that left his press. A printer would, on the other hand, keep in his shop trade copies of his work, bound either by himself or by someone he was accustomed to employ, though he did not necessarily keep a binder on his own staff. For this reason, there are styles of binding decoration associated with some of these early printers. Caxton's binder, whom Pollard believes to have been Flemish, and whom he identifies as one Jacobus Bokebynder who, in 1495, leased the shop next to the one that had been Caxton's (the printer is believed to have died *ca.* 1491),[33] liked to divide his field into lozenge-shaped compartments, a single stamp being placed in the center of each. Designs based on diagonals forming lozenges became typical of books bound in England at the time, which is not the same as saying that the design was English.

The economic aspects of bookbinding are more difficult to assess, since much depended upon the size, purpose, and ownership of the books involved, and these considerations do not necessarily show in the records concerning money actually paid. There could, for instance, be nothing typical about the expensive original binding of the Lytlington Missal of Westminster Abbey, made at the end of the fourteenth century. The records show breakdowns as follows: "for sewing (*ligacione*), 21s; for covering (*coopertura*), 8d; for embroidery (*broudura*), 6s; for 6 knots (*nodulis*), 12s; for a jewel (*baga*), 4s. 6d."[34] H. E. Bell, in his study of binding costs, gives some interesting averages. The average cost

◈§ *Of "bookes, clad in blak or reed"*

of binding eighty-one service books between 1340 and 1540 was 3s. 3d.; of twenty-eight other books between the same dates, 1s. 6d. This, of course, implies that service books got the best bindings that could be afforded. More specifically, Bell notes that the common leather and board bindings of two Cambridge manuscripts (Peterhouse 114 and 154) cost 2s. each.[35] Binders might also receive time rates. In 1396, a binder at Ely received 4s. for two weeks' work, though his time may well have been occupied with repairs.[36]

The purpose of this study has been to review typical medieval bookbinding and structure as they existed in Chaucer's lifetime and in the century following. We may speculate that a famous author might have owned handsome and valuable books, and that he had his own library treasures bound or rebound, perhaps expensively, to suit his personal taste. Most, however, of the volumes still in their original, or at least medieval, bindings testify that English books of the time were, for the greater part, modest productions. As for the Clerk of Oxford's shelf of Aristotles, there is no reason to assign them bindings of any extravagant cost in view of the recorded prices of other books modestly bound. Of university books, however, there will be more to say in a later chapter.[37]

NOTES TO CHAPTER I

[1]See below, pp. 90-92.

[2]The rapid decay of modern leather bookbindings is the subject of an investigation by a committee representing the Society of Arts and the Worshipful Company of Leathersellers, *Report of the Committee on Leather for Bookbinding*, ed. Charles George Lyttleton, 8th viscount Cobham, and Henry Trueman Wood (London, 1905).

[3]Vespasiano da Bisticci, *The Vespasiano Memoirs*, trans. William George and Emily Waters (London, 1926), p. 104.

[4]Bindings are included in the descriptions of manuscripts given by John Matthews Manly and Edith Rickert, *The Text of the Canterbury Tales*

(Chicago, 1940), I, 29-544, hereafter cited as M-R. All further references to descriptions of manuscripts of the *Canterbury Tales* are to M-R unless otherwise specified.

[5]*The Oxford English Dictionary* (Oxford, 1933), XII, 86.

[6]See also G. S. Ivy, "The Bibliography of the Manuscript Book," in *The English Library before 1700*, ed. Francis Wormald and Cyril E. Wright (London, 1958), p. 35. The foliation is inaccurately reported.

[7]Hedwig Saxl, "Histology of Parchment," *Technical Studies in the Field of the Fine Arts* (Harvard Univ.: the William Hayes Fogg Art Museum), 8 (1939-40), 3-9.

[8]Ivy, "Bibliography of the Manuscript Book," pp. 34-36. See also *Encyclopaedia Britannica*, 14th ed. (Chicago, 1969), III, 921-22; XVII, 337-38.

[9]Curt Ferdinand Bühler, *The Fifteenth-Century Book* (Philadelphia, 1960), p. 42.

[10]Dard Hunter, *Papermaking*, 2nd ed., rev. (New York, 1957), p. 5.

[11]The authoritative work on watermarks is Charles Moïse Briquet, *Les Filigranes*, 2nd ed. (1923, rpt. New York, 1966).

[12]Hunter, *Papermaking*, p. 229.

[13]*A History of Agriculture and Prices in England* (Oxford, 1866-1902), I, 643-45. For discussion of money and prices in medieval England, see below, pp. 140-54. For photographs of coins, see Plate I.

[14]Ed. Walter William Skeat, 2nd ed. (Edinburgh, 1911).

[15]*The Paston Letters.* A.D. *1422-1509*, ed. James Gairdner, new ed. (London, 1904), V, 3.

[16]Rogers, *Agriculture and Prices*, I, 643-45. See also Ronald Edward Zupko, *A Dictionary of English Weights and Measures* (Madison, Wisc., 1968), pp. 155-56.

[17]*The Life and Typography of William Caxton* (London, 1861-63), II, xx-xxi. See also below, pp. 143-44, 146.

[18]For a complete discussion of the gatherings of the manuscripts of the *Canterbury Tales*, see M-R, I, 13-18, and passim. Excellent descriptions of the manuscripts may also be found in William Symington McCormick and Janet E. Heseltine, *The Manuscripts of Chaucer's "Canterbury Tales"* (Oxford, 1933).

[19]A full description of Add. MS. 5140 is given by M-R, I, 29-33.

[20]The sewing frame is still used in hand-binding. For illustration, see

Edith Diehl, *Bookbinding* (New York, 1946), II, 123; see also *Encyclopaedia Britannica*, III, Plate 6 (1).

[21] Graham Pollard, "The Construction of English Twelfth-Century Bindings," *The Library*, 5th Ser., 17 (1962), 8-9. Diagrams and photographs are included. Pollard also says in a study of fifteenth-century bindings that in some cases the boards were planed along with the gatherings in one operation, though how this is possible is not clear: "The Names of Some English Fifteenth-Century Binders," *The Library*, 5th Ser., 25 (1970), 198.

[22] Pollard, "Twelfth-Century Bindings," passim.

[23] Described by M-R, I, 48-51.

[24] Pollard, "Twelfth-Century Bindings," p. 13.

[25] Described by M-R, I, 289-94.

[26] Pollard, "Twelfth-Century Bindings," p. 22.

[27] Ibid., pp. 15-16.

[28] See below, pp. 127-128.

[29] Described by M-R, I, 421-26.

[30] Ernst Philipp Goldschmidt, *Gothic & Renaissance Bookbindings* (London, 1928), I, 16.

[31] Described by M-R, I, 494-500.

[32] Geoffrey Dudley Hobson, *English Binding Before 1500* (Cambridge, 1929), pp. 2, 14.

[33] Pollard, "Fifteenth-Century Binders," pp. 205-206. Hobson (Plates 42-44 and p. 19), among others, believes that Caxton had two binders.

[34] Joseph Armitage Robinson and Montague Rhodes James, eds., *The Manuscripts of Westminster Abbey* (Cambridge, 1909), pp. 7-8. The knots must have been mountings for jewels, for the costs seem high.

[35] "The Price of Books in Medieval England," *The Library*, 4th Ser., 17 (1937), 321.

[36] Ibid., p. 316.

[37] See below, pp. 90-92.

2

Pictures and Decoration in Books

MANUSCRIPTS THEMSELVES, even more than their bindings, presented wonderful opportunities to medieval artists, and their work ranges from decorated initials to illuminated "miniatures." Medieval manuscripts almost always have, at minimum, colored initials at the beginnings of sections. In the late fifteenth century woodcut became widely used as a method of providing artwork for both manuscripts and printed books. Since Chaucer studies inevitably bring one into contact with manuscript art it is necessary to know something about this subject.

The expression "manuscript art" has been employed so that more technical terms can be introduced and explained. "Illumination" is so frequently used as a general term for manuscript painting that it is pointless to offer a more restricted definition, in which the pages are described as lighted up with bright colors and burnished with gold or silver leaf,[1] and the term will be used here in the general sense. The art of illumination has, at least theoretically, two major aspects: illustration and decoration. Illustration refers to the use of pictures to explicate a text. Illustration was practiced by the Greeks and Romans in scientific treatises, although since almost no original examples are extant, their work is now known only through late classical and early medieval copies. Decoration can refer to any nonillustrative art appearing upon the page. It pertains chiefly to the ornamentation of initial letters, to columns and capitals often used to contain lists and tables, and to borders or partial borders. Pictures in manuscripts are known as "miniatures." The term has nothing to do with size; it comes from the

Pictures and Decorations in Books

Latin *minium*, the oxide of lead used by the Romans in the preparation of red (*rubum*, whence 'rubric,' something written in red). In practice, miniatures are not necessarily small, some of them occupying whole pages of large manuscripts.

From treatises written in the fourteenth and fifteenth centuries, it is evident that artists went to extraordinary pains to obtain the most elementary materials of their profession, such as brushes and fixatives a modern painter has only to buy and use. The ingredients and preparation of colors were highly personal matters with the individual artist, protected by tradition, their worth and lasting qualities often proved by the passage of time. There is entertainment value in reading some of these treatises with their recipes for colors and other materials, recipes that now seem strange. One learns that fishglue is made by boiling the stomach of a sturgeon; that blue is produced from lapis lazuli; that another blue is made from fermented seeds, their juice absorbed into linen and dried in a dark place over boxes of earth soaked in urine. The most famous treatise on techniques and materials is that of Cennino Cennini, who was living in Padua in 1398.[2] How much Chaucer knew about these matters it is impossible to say. Nor is there any measure of what he may have encountered in the way of really ancient manuscripts. But, widely traveled and well-read as he was, it must be assumed that he was a connoisseur of fine books, and that he knew more than most people of the time about manuscript art.

While there are no extant contemporary manuscripts of Chaucer's works, the artwork in some fifteenth-century manuscripts tells much about him and about his admirers. His portraits, one of which accompanies manuscripts of Hoccleve's *Regement of Princes*, are meant not only to decorate the books that contain them, but to honor Chaucer and to preserve his likeness.[3] As for the Chaucer manuscripts, being a cross section of vernacular books, they are a commentary on the kind of book art Englishmen wanted in their day. One of the most interesting aspects of this is the fact that those who commissioned the Ellesmere Manuscript, the most famous and the most luxurious of all, selected an atelier which worked, not in the more fashionable International Style, but in the conservative, English traditions of East Anglian art. The choice cannot fail to impress Chaucer's present-day readers, for no gallery of characters outside of Shakespeare and Dickens has ever seemed so thoroughly English as the company that assembled at the Tabard. One of course wonders whether the style was chosen for similar reasons. While the question cannot be answered, it is obvious that any discussion of books as Chaucer knew them, and as they were known to his earliest editors, requires a context in the history of manuscript painting in England.[4]

The story of manuscript painting proper to Chaucer's milieu of books begins after the Norman Conquest, with the period of Romanesque art, which, in its own way, England shared with the rest of western Europe.[5] A major contributing factor to the development of Romanesque painting was the reentry of Byzantine traditions into the European artstream, through Norman Sicily and through Constantinople under the Crusades. Its impact shows in art in many ways, but noteworthy is a movement toward large scale and magnificence. Miniatures were treated as framed compositions with painted or gilded backgrounds, and drawn figures became monumental, appearing larger than life regardless of actual size. There is in Romanesque productions a quest for movement, and an attempt to occupy every available space. Art historians call this allover design *horror vacui*. Sometimes human and animal figures are contorted into fantastic shapes to fit into the open spaces within initials. The most important twelfth-century English book with regard to artwork is the Winchester Bible, 23 x 15¼ inches in size, its artwork begun in the last quarter of the century.[6] No fewer than six artists worked on the manuscript, all anonymous and now known by such sobriquets as "the Master of the Leaping Figures," "the Master of the Apocryphal Figures," "the Master of the Morgan Leaf," and "the Master of the Gothic Majesty." Best known among secular manuscripts of the time are "bestiaries," allegories of animals, real or imaginary, and their habits.[7]

Animal figures, taken from bestiaries and from nature, became especially characteristic of English manuscript art in the thirteenth

Pictures and Decorations in Books

century, as did a penchant for animal grotesques, which came to be used as caricatures of human frailties. These trends coincided with a development in book production which was to have a great impact upon the art of illumination. Secularization was becoming a powerful force in that society, and books were increasingly for laymen, who wanted not only romances and other secular fare but also personal copies of the Psalter. Also in demand were books containing the Hours of the Virgin and the Office of the Dead. Such volumes are known under various names: primers, books of hours, *horae*.[8] Vital here was an increasing demand for portability. Once small size had become an ideal as well as a practical objective, ideal writing material had to be thin and became marvelously so, while art, severely curtailed in space, became exquisite rather than grand.

In adapting their art to the restrictions of small pages, illuminators became especially interested in historiated initials, initials incorporating miniatures in their design. These paintings were often made to terminate in a stiff, tail-like appendage, which extended into the margin, sometimes for considerable length, and ended in a knob or leaf. A development of this was its extension, turning the corners, into a bar border, surrounding all or part of the text. By *ca.* 1300, one finds the rigidity relieved by curves and foliage, and the bar soon becomes a luxurious, leafy border, decorated with flowers, fruit, birds, animals, and, especially in England, grotesques. Decorated borders and partial borders were called "vinets" (vignettes) and "demi-vinets," and they are still known by these names. *Bas de page* scenes from daily life sometimes appear between the last line of the text and the border. These small books could and did contain other miniatures besides historiated initials and *bas de page* scenes. A favorite method of production was to arrange a number of miniatures together on a single page, which was divided into compartments, often richly framed, for the purpose.

This is, of course, the Gothic book art of the later Middle Ages. The technical differences between Romanesque and Gothic art are admirably discussed by Erwin Panofsky.[9] The whole impression of Gothic miniature painting is luxurious and delicate, rather than grand and monumental. This is not to suggest, however, that large books were passé. Sanctuary books had to be large to be read by more than one person at a time, and to be read from a standing position. As for privately owned library treasures, not all collectors wanted their valuable manuscripts produced on a small scale, and some of the most famous are large indeed. The first celebrated artist of very small books was Jean Pucelle, who lived in Paris in the second quarter of the fourteenth century. He and the disciples of his atelier are especially noted for books of hours.

Turning to Chaucer's England: East Anglian artists dominated the first half of his century and were influential abroad. East Anglia was then the commercial center of England, its seaports directly across the Channel from the Low Countries. This connection with the Low Countries is important, for it may have been the presence in East Anglia of foreign artists, especially Flemish, which gave impetus to the rich development of art there.

Whether a native development or something under impact from abroad, if not both, East Anglian scriptoria produced handsome manuscripts with common characteristics: rich borders, filled with the things of nature—leaves, flowers, birds, and animals; proliferation of grotesques, producing a bizarre combination of naturalism and the absurd; the addition of *bas de page* scenes and drawings in the margins, the subjects taken from many sources. If the art in these manuscripts is sometimes overblown, it is nevertheless interesting and full of life. One especially characteristic feature is the recurring presence of the English daisy. Gold is plentiful, diapered or otherwise decorated. Famous products of East Anglian scriptoria are the Gorleston[10] and Luttrell psalters, the latter a rich quarry for modern illustrators of books on the Middle Ages because of its *bas de page* scenes from everyday life.[11] Notable also is the Psalter of Queen Mary, so named because it was seized by a customs official from someone trying to export it and presented to Mary Tudor. Its 320 leaves are rich, even crowded, with miniatures, consisting of tinted drawings as well as of others lavish with gold.[12] Plate IV shows the E-page of a *Beatus vir* sequence illustrating the beginning of Psalm I, from an East Anglian psalter of the late thirteenth century in the Pierpont Morgan Library. The book is known as the *Windmill Psalter* because the unknown artist included a windmill among other specimens of local color in his design.

The vigor of East Anglian art ended in mid-century, due perhaps to the Black Death, as some have thought, or simply to its own lack of further inspiration. The productive years of Chaucer's career correspond with the period when painters all over Europe were moving toward the International Style, a confluence of Italian styles of the early *Trecento*, chiefly Sienese, and northern Gothic styles,[13] which reached its most perfect expression in the so-called *Très Riches Heures* made for the Duc de Berry and painted by the Flemish Limbourg brothers, 1413-16.[14]

This development is rooted in the fact that certain Sienese painters, most notably Duccio, had chosen to work under the influence of Byzantine traditions which had lingered in Italy since the siege of Constantinople (1204). Their most important contribution to art is the fact that they learned to place figures together in the interiors of buildings, showing them as if through a window frame by the expedient of removing the front wall. This development led to the eventual conquest of perspective in the fifteenth century, in the work of the Flemish masters Jan van Eyck and Roger van der Weyden. The style of Duccio and his followers was widely influential in the principal cultural centers of western Europe, developing in each case its own blend with the local Gothic art.

England, which was no longer in a position of leadership in art after the decline of East Anglian style, was particularly receptive to foreign influences in the second half of the century. Italian influence even before that has been well described by Otto Pächt as characterized not only by the world of the Sienese painters, but also by that of Giotto, with his massive figures seen from foreshortened backviews and other positions that would have been impossible to earlier painters.[15] French, Flemish, and Bohemian influences are seen in English painting of Chaucer's time, the latter particularly evidenced in the 1380s, a reflection of the politi-

PLATE IV (Gothic)
in consilio impiorum: *et* in uia pec
catorum non stetit: *et* in cathedra pe
stilentie non sedit.
Sed in lege domini uoluntas eius:
5   *et* in lege eius meditabitur die ac nocte.
Et erit tanquam lignum q*uo*d plan
tatum est secus decursus aquaru*m*:

Notes: Separated words occur at the ends of lines 1, 2, and 6. There is no modern equivalent of the *punctus elevatus*, here represented by a colon.

Pictures and Decorations in Books

PLATE IV. A page from an East Anglian psalter of the late thirteenth century

cal and cultural ties accompanying the marriage of Richard II and Anne of Bohemia. The best example of English painting done under Bohemian influence is the coronation book of Westminster Abbey *(Liber Regalis)* made *ca.* 1382. The miniature shown by Margaret Rickert is in a stiff border decorated with East Anglian daisy buds, but the figures have long, tapering bodies and enormous hands.[16]

Some generalizations can be made about the International Style. As a phase in the history of art, it must be described as mannerist: that is, as having certain self-conscious exaggerations. These may take the form of figures with rather elongated bodies, and of clothes shown with exceedingly meticulous attention to detail, such as embroidery and jewelry. This art is aristocratic, but at the same time it delights in a naturalism which shows peasants engaged in homespun activities that support the nobility. In this sense, there is an indebtedness to the *bas de page* art of the East Anglian period, which liked to show scenes from everyday life and especially to illustrate the seasons. The English masterpieces of the International Style are the Wilton Diptych, with its kneeling figure of the young Richard II, so genuinely international that art historians are still debating the provenience of its artist or artists,[17] and the missal made for the Carmelites of London, one of its three artists being Dutch. This work has been reconstructed from fragments by Margaret Rickert.[18]

In a discussion of this kind, general trends in style are more important than descriptive lists of specific works, for, as is well known, the accident of survival is not necessarily a measure of the reputation a work enjoyed in its own day. Nor is there any measure, other than general trends, of Chaucer's personal knowledge of illumination. There can be no reasonable doubt, however, that a man of books was aware of the mainstream of style in miniature painting; that a man of literature who had been at least twice to Italy knew something about *Trecento* styles; and that a poet who served Richard II knew that Bohemian painting had influence upon contemporary art in his own country. It is also reasonable

Pictures and Decorations in Books

to suppose that Chaucer was well aware of the characteristics of East Anglian miniature painting, which represented conservative English tradition in painting.

As for the artists who worked in manuscript illumination, English ateliers were rarely conducive to fame. But the names of a few notable English miniature painters are indeed known. There are two important artists from the thirteenth century: Matthew Paris, a monk of St. Albans *ca.* 1217, who was also a chronicler,[19] and W. de Brailes, who left several signed self-portraits among his works and who may have been the William de Brailes mentioned in some Oxford documents *ca.* 1230-60.[20] The art of Matthew Paris is typical of English outline drawing, which may be lightly tinted, such as one meets even before the Norman Conquest.[21] Interest in draftsmanship is one of the important characteristics of English painting throughout the Middle Ages.

Best known now among painters of Chaucer's time or slightly later are John Siferwas and Herman Scheere. Siferwas, thought to be of English birth despite his foreign name, painted his portrait in a lectionary made for his patron, John, Lord Lovell (d. 1408), and he was also the principal artist of the Sherborne Missal.[22] Herman Scheere was probably a native of Ghent. He left a larger corpus of works than Siferwas. Some of the miniatures of his atelier are readily recognized by the motto, appearing all or in part, "Si quis amat non laborat. Omnia levia sunt amanti."[23] Scheere was influenced by the Italian *Trecento*, except that he espoused the English preference for draftsmanship, so that his work is chiefly two-dimensional. Margaret Rickert attributes to him two miniatures in a Brussels manuscript (Bib. Roy. MS. 4862-4864, fols. 66^b-67) which contains, among other items, Chaucer's *Treatise on the Astrolabe*.[24] While Miss Rickert's conclusion that the manuscript could have been copied in the fourteenth century is contradicted by the fact that the *Treatise* is unfinished, Herman Scheere is the one important miniaturist whose name can be associated with a Chaucer manuscript.

Both Siferwas and Scheere could have seen Chaucer. Although

there is no evidence connecting either of them with the poet, there are seven portraits in manuscripts dating before 1500, either claiming to represent Chaucer or assumed to do so:

> MS. Harley 4866, British Museum (Hoccleve's *Regement of Princes*, written in 1411-12), fol. 91: half length.
>
> MS. Royal 17. D. vi, British Museum (first quarter, fifteenth century. Hoccleve's *Regement of Princes*), fol. 90b: full length.
>
> MS. Lansdowne 851, British Museum (reign of Henry V; *Canterbury Tales*), fol. 2: historiated initial, full length.
>
> MS. Ellesmere, Huntington Library (1400-10: *Canterbury Tales*), fol. 157b: equestrian (Plate V).
>
> MS. 61, Corpus Christi College, Cambridge (early fifteenth century: *Troilus and Criseyde*), fol. 1b: standing, behind a lectern, in an outdoor pulpit (Plate VI).
>
> MS. Bodley 686, Bodleian Library (1430-40: *Canterbury Tales*), fol. 1: historiated initial, full length.
>
> MS. Devonshire (privately owned; 1450-60: *Canterbury Tales*), fol. 1: historiated initial, full length, seated.

Margaret Rickert, whose association with the Manly-Edith Rickert work on the *Canterbury Tales* would have been conducive to a discussion of all the Chaucer portraits, including others not considered here which are panel paintings, did not expand her study in that work beyond the manuscripts there presented,[25] and she adds little in her own fine study of painting in Britain. The standard study of the Chaucer portraits therefore remains that of M. H. Spielmann (1900), which is incomplete and at times less than clear.[26]

The oldest and most important of the manuscripts involved is the Ellesmere copy of the *Canterbury Tales*, which, as is well known, contains in the margin, next to the beginning of each tale, an equestrian portrait of its pilgrim narrator.[27] It is this format which regrettably prevented the artist from including the host, Harry Bailly. More than one artist worked at the drawings: at

◄§ *Pictures and Decorations in Books*

least three, though there may have been more. As analyzed by Herbert C. Schulz, the work of the several artists may be seen as follows:

1. The portrait of Chaucer (4" in height; fol. 153^b).
2. The Monk, Nun's Priest, Second Nun, Canon's Yeoman, and Manciple (2¾" to 3⅞" in height; fols. 169, 179, 194, 203).
3. The remaining portraits, which are the work of either one artist or two working in the same style (1⅞" to 2⅞" in height; the Knight 3¾").

The chief distinction between the work of the second artist and that of the third is that the second includes plots of grass for his horses to stand upon, whereas the third artist does not.

The personality and dress of the figures are close to the descriptions given by Chaucer in the "General Prologue." The horses, too, looking rather pleased with themselves (especially Chaucer's), follow the descriptions, down to the ribs of the Clerk's mangy nag. It is interesting that at least three of the horses (those of the Franklin, Shipman, and Squire) have been traced with a stylus. This fact is revealed by deep indentations in the pages. The riders were drawn in after the horses were painted. That the drawings were executed before the gatherings were bound is evidenced, not only from usual practice, but from the marks left by the tracing in the Franklin's portrait, which have gone through to the preceding two leaves of the manuscript (the first two in their gathering), but not beyond.[28] The portraits can be seen in color in the facsimile edition of the manuscript, with the difference that the inside margin was widened in preparing the facsimile, the outer margin reduced, so that the pages could be seen more clearly.

The custom of illustrating manuscripts of the *Canterbury Tales* with portraits of the pilgrims was not confined to the Ellesmere copy. MS. Gg. 4. 27 (1420-40) of Cambridge University was supplied with portraits in the same manner, six of the originals surviving in similar positions: the Reeve, Cook, Wife of Bath, Pardoner, Monk, and Manciple.[29] Torn leaves show that the set was originally complete. These pictures, while far from the quality of the Ellesmere drawings, need not be described as poor, for they have the appearance of satire, especially the horses. The two "Oxford fragments," owned respectively by the John Rylands Library, Manchester (two leaves: Rylands English MS. 63) and by the Philip H. and A.S.W. Rosenbach Foundation, Philadelphia (eleven leaves), contain between them three miniatures (the Miller, Cook, Man of Law), and there is no reason to suppose that the artist originally limited himself to these.[30] MS. Harley 1758 of the British Museum provides spaces for miniatures which were never supplied.[31]

In addition to the portraits, one other type of miniature occurs in Gg: allegorical representations of vices and virtues, used as illustrations of the Parson's tale, though without basis in Chaucer's own text. Only three of them remain, the other four having been destroyed with pages torn out of the manuscript. The miniatures, which occupy a third to a half of their pages, are pairs of figures: Envy and Charity (fol. 416), Gluttony and Abstinence (fol. 432), Lechery and Chastity (fol. 433).[32] Since the manuscript was copied 1420-40, and since there is no reason to suppose that the miniatures were added any later, the artist's precedents were in literature and art earlier than those dates. One literary precedent is Gower's *Mirour de l'Omme* (841-948), where vices are described as riding upon mythical animals.[33]

In Gg, the beasts of the vices (wolf, bear, and goat, respectively), and the symbols carried or worn by the figures, who are themselves rather neutral, carry the allegory. The symbols of the vices, who are for some reason all male whereas the virtues are female, are: knife and lash; kite; and sparrow, respectively. The virtues, standing figures wearing the nimbus, carry or wear the following symbols: flaming, winged heart, sceptre, and triple crown; crown, pitcher, and flower; and cross-headed spear piercing the head of a beast on which the figure is standing. The virtues all have robes which fall at the feet symmetrically, in the manner of a fishtail.

Pictures and Decorations in Books

With regard to the miniatures in Gg, Rickert sees the work of two hands:

1. Reeve, Cook, Wife of Bath, Pardoner (fols. 186-306).
2. Monk, Manciple, Envy/Charity, Gluttony/Abstinence, Lechery/Chastity (fols. 352-433).

The allegorical figures, in other words, are by the second artist.[34]

The bases for distinguishing the two artists are the facial types and the modeling techniques, as well as the different styles in drawing the horses. The latter, as done by the first artist, have long, thin necks and large feet, at times with unusually short legs. All have grotesque eyes. The two cart horses drawn by the second artist are as odd as the first lot, but they are distinguished by more realistic portrayal of flesh, bone, and muscle. With regard to the figures as drawn by the first artist, the flesh is white, the features indicated by brown lines, the mouths and cheeks by red dabs. The eyes are small and heavy-lidded, the far eye being higher than the nearer. The second artist was better at modeling than the first, the most distinguishing characteristic being heavy eyebrows and dark circles under the eyes. There is shading around the jaw and chin.[35] The allegorical figures would doubtless receive more attention from Chaucer scholars if they were specifically representative of descriptions supplied by Chaucer himself.

Returning to the Ellesmere Manuscript: the portrait of Chaucer was evidently intended to be the highlight of its series, for the artist in charge of the project built up to it by withholding major decoration from the "Sir Thopas" page, where Chaucer's role as a pilgrim narrator actually begins, and the portrait is placed instead at the beginning of the "Melibee," which, it will be recalled, Chaucer offers as more worthy fare when he is called down for his tail-rime imitation of popular romance. The poet appears, not only pointing to his lines, but somewhat larger than his companions, this apparently not the result of the artist's idea of emphasis but the result of problems in composition. Alone among the portraits, Chaucer's is out of proportion, the torso having been short-

Chaucer and the Medieval Book

PLATE V. Portrait of Chaucer from the Ellesmere Manuscript of the *Canterbury Tales*

◆§ Pictures and Decorations in Books

ened below the belt to fit a horse, drawn or traced on a smaller scale. Since the artists responsible for the other portraits produced reasonably proportioned figures, the most obvious explanation is that Chaucer's was adapted from an already existing portrait to the equestrian pose (Plate V).

This matter becomes the more interesting when the Ellesmere portrait is compared with that which appears in Harleian MS. 4866 (fol. 91), a manuscript of Hoccleve's *Regement of Princes*, together with the following stanza (4992-98),

> Al thogh his lyfe be queynt the resemblaunce
> Of him hath in me so fressh lyflynesse
> That to putte othir men in remembraunce
> Of his p*er*sone I have heere his lyknesse
> Do make to this ende in sothfastnesse
> That thei *that* have of him lest thought *and* mynde
> By this peynture may ageyn him fynde.[36]

Hoccleve, who must have seen Chaucer and who certainly admired him, makes a very simple claim: he has had a true likeness of the poet put into his manuscript, though the exact circumstances are not known now—as, for instance, whether it was copied from an original or drawn from memory for the first time in his manuscript. There is good reason to suppose that it was copied from an original, for it differs little from the torso of the portrait in the older Ellesmere MS., in which Chaucer is apparently wearing the same clothes, although his hand holds the horse's reins instead of beads and although the two portraits face opposite directions. This, however, is not enough to indicate different sources, for one pose can be derived from the other, more or less, with a mirror and with a few simple changes. A poorer version of the Hoccleve portrait, oriented as in the Ellesmere Manuscript but showing the figure standing, with oddly deformed feet, appears in a second manuscript of the *Regement of Princes*, Royal MS. 17. D. vi (fol. 90ᵇ) of the British Museum.[37] A third, presumably based on one of these, has been cut out of Harleian MS.

43

4866, also of the British Museum, which contains Hoccleve's poem.

William A. Shaw has proposed that one Richard Herman, a king's clerk and chaplain, painted the portrait of Chaucer in Hoccleve's manuscript,[38] but this does not account for its similarity to the Ellesmere miniature, which may be as much as a decade older and which, as noted, appears to have been adapted from an already existing portrait. While it is known that Richard II had a court painter, Gilbert Prince, now identified only from numerous records that show him to have been busy and well paid, there is no evidence that he ever painted a portrait of Chaucer.[39] Whatever their origin, the two miniatures stand up well against the literary projection of himself—his persona—that Chaucer delights in placing before the reader in the *Canterbury Tales* and elsewhere. The persona, of course, is a fictionalized Chaucer, intended, as E. T. Donaldson has ably shown, to admit the poet, a commoner, to an aristocratic audience by speaking instead of Chaucer himself. To accomplish this, the poet has exploited his physical personality, plump and affable, though there is no reason to suppose that the real Chaucer was the simple fellow who puts forth "Sir Thopas."[40] Thus, in some ways Chaucer himself provides a portrait, and, whatever one may believe about the intent of the persona, there is no conflict with the two miniatures that have been discussed. On the contrary, there is much to support the conclusion that the unknown painter indeed presented a true likeness of Chaucer, as Hoccleve claims in the *Regement of Princes*.

Other miniatures representing Chaucer are imaginary portraits. That in MS. 61, Corpus Christi College, Cambridge (fol. 1ᵇ) shows characteristics of the International Style. A man stands in an outdoor pulpit before an assembly of lords and ladies, gathered in front of a lacy castle, which resembles a French château. The castle stands on a hill, overlooking another one in the distance on a pinnacle of Italianate rocks. The whole scene is lavishly painted and luxurious. The modeling of the figures in the foreground, some of whom assume rather massive seated postures reminiscent of Giotto, contrasts with the delicate details in some of the cos-

Pictures and Decorations in Books

PLATE VI. Portrait of Chaucer from an early fifteenth-century manuscript

tumes. Were the miniature anywhere but in a copy of *Troilus and Criseyde*, no one would suppose that the insignificant, bearded man in the pulpit is Chaucer, the royal couple nearby Richard II and Queen Anne (Plate VI).[41]

Three historiated initials are additional examples of this kind of portraiture rather than of that of the Hoccleve and Ellesmere portraits. These are in MSS. Lansdowne 851 of the British Museum, fol. 2; Bodley 686 of the Bodleian Library, fol. 1; and Devonshire (privately owned), fol. 1.[42] All stand in the initial *W* of the "General Prologue," as one undoubtedly did in MS. Rawlinson Poetry 223 of the Bodleian Library, which has other historiated initials but which has lost its first leaf. The Lansdowne miniature shows Chaucer full-length, standing, and holding an open book from which he appears to be reading. He wears a long grey gown, but instead of the familiar headdress his hair is shown cropped (anachronistically) in the manner fashionable in the mid-fifteenth century. He appears as a much younger man than the subject of the Ellesmere and Hoccleve portraits. A pen case is fastened to his gown.

The figure of the Bodleian manuscript is probably meant to be Chaucer also, though Margaret Rickert suspects that he may instead represent the patron for whom the manuscript was made. Here the subject holds a red hat and gestures with his left hand. He wears a knee-length gown of blue trimmed with dark fur. His sleeves are full at the shoulder in the fashion of the 1430s, and his hair is cut in the style shown in the Lansdowne miniature, but, in contrast with that portrait, there is no beard. In the Devonshire Manuscript, the figure is seated, his head supported by his right hand while he gestures with his left. There is again some suggestion that the patron, rather than Chaucer, may be the subject of the miniature, but the position at the beginning of the *Canterbury Tales* would argue otherwise. The gown in this case is red, full-length, trimmed with fur, and belted. The figure wears a tall hat.

Miniatures are, of course, only part of the illumination that appears in manuscripts. Here a distinction needs to be made: between illustrative art and minor embellishment of the calligraphy,

Pictures and Decorations in Books

which, while undeniably art even as handwriting itself is a species of art, belongs to that specialized area rather than to a study of illumination. Thus, the most common use of color in medieval manuscripts—usually, though not always, red or blue—is for paragraph marks and for ordinary initials at the beginnings of works and of their divisions. Known as rubrication, this work was done after the copying was finished, the scribe having left guide marks in the appropriate places. The scribe might do this finishing himself, but it was ordinarily left to a specialist, known as a rubrisher or rubricator, whose services were also required by printers before they began to use woodcut initials. Sometimes initials were pen-flourished with contrasting colors or with gold. Initials, however, were frequently given special treatment as artistic compositions. An initial done in gold on a colored ground, having sprays attached to its outer corners which may or may not become vinets, was called "champ," a name still used for this type of illumination. A further step in initial art is the historiated initial, which, as discussed earlier, incorporates a miniature in its design.

Apart from the miniatures, Margaret Rickert has identified three basic patterns in the arrangement of the artwork in illuminated manuscripts of the *Canterbury Tales* as follows:

1. Vinets and/or demi-vinets for the principal divisions, champs for the secondary (14 MSS).
2. Vinets and/or demi-vinets for the principal divisions, pen-flourished initials of varying sizes for the secondary (9 MSS).
3. Champs for the principal divisions, pen-flourished initials for the secondary (5 MSS).[43]

The importance of these patterns is not so much their classification of artwork in manuscripts that happen to represent the *Canterbury Tales*. As noted earlier, other works by Chaucer, and works by other English poets, reside in some of the same books, and, since there are so many of them, the real significance of the classification is that it shows trends through a cross section of English vernacular manuscripts of the fifteenth century ranging from

Chaucer and the Medieval Book

the truly luxurious to the relatively modest. Since the trends show more in vinets and demi-vinets than in champs, Rickert's analysis of style is based on the twenty-three manuscripts belonging to the first and second categories of her classification. Her findings may be summarized as follows:

Group I (1400-15).
    A. Conservative tradition (East Anglian). Stiff bar border, with branches curling into a stiff scroll with hair-line pen flourishes, which are sometimes tipped with gold balls alternating with colored trefoils. The bar is frequently ornamented with interlaced knots. Oak leaves and flower forms appear: daisy buds, marigolds, and wild roses. Principal colors: pink, blue, dull red, green, gold.

       MSS: Hengwrt, National Library of Wales
            Ellesmere, Huntington Library (Plate VII)

    B. Newer style. Bar border at the top and bottom margins drawn into a slender hairline spray decorated with small green dots. More motifs are added, giving a more naturalistic appearance. The innovations are all in the sprays, the bar border remaining stiff and heavy, with conventional trefoliate motifs.

       MSS: Harley 4334, British Museum
            Lansdowne 851, British Museum
            Corpus Christi College 198, Oxford.

Group II (1430-50)
    Acanthus scroll attached to the top or bottom of the bar, changing the concept of a branch growing into sprays. Large flower motifs finish the bar ends, offering new points of attachment for sprays. More green dots, often modified into drops, decorate the sprays.

       MSS: Petworth (National Trust)
            Egerton 2863, British Museum
            Lichfield Cathedral 2
            Phillipps 8137 (privately owned)
            Mm. 2. 5, Cambridge University
            Delamere (privately owned)

⋙ *Pictures and Decorations in Books*

Oxford; two fragments owned respectively by the John Rylands Library, Manchester (two leaves: Rylands English MS. 63) and by the Philip H. and A.S.W. Rosenbach Foundation, Philadelphia (eleven leaves)

Group III (1430-50)

Longer, thinner sprays, dividing backward and forward in the manner of a Greek scroll, the interstices filled with green dots and pen flourishes. Self-shaded, almost three-dimensional motifs, placed at the tip of each curving branch, forming a center to it. This type of spray shows a French influence, itself influenced by Italian shading technique.

MSS: Bodley 686, Bodleian Library
 Laud 600, Bodleian Library

Group IV (1450-60)

Arrangement of sprays to form a band, as in MS. Bodley 686, but differing from Group III in flatness and conventionality of the motifs, harshness of colors, and coarseness of design.

MSS: Harley 1758, British Museum
 Hatton Donat 1, Bodleian Library
 Selden Arch. B. 14, Bodleian Library

Group V (1450-70)

Large manuscripts, probably produced by the same shop. Feathery spray surrounding a stiff bar border, the spray sometimes with its flora turned back against itself, giving a tangled impression.

MSS: R. 3. 3, Trinity College, Cambridge
 Rawlinson Poetry 223, Bodleian Library
 Devonshire (privately owned)

Group VI (end fifteenth century)

Structurally rigid. Simple motifs, large in proportion, with conventional shading.

MSS: Additional 5140, British Museum
 Longleat 257 (privately owned)[44]

It is interesting to realize that the most luxurious of these manuscripts, the Ellesmere, follows the conservative English tradition of East Anglia, even though it is thought to have been produced in London, for East Anglian art cannot have been fashionable in the first decade of the fifteenth century, which was the day of the International Style.

Painting and book art were soon to differentiate themselves, not because of printing, as is so widely supposed, but because painting was already beginning to free itself from the parchment and vellum surface when the Wilton Diptych was made. Panel painting begins to replace the manuscript miniature for important art, especially portraiture, in the fifteenth century, while the manuscript miniature reaches a new development under printing: namely, woodcut.[45]

There is less of a gap between manuscripts and their artwork and the earliest printed books, known as incunabula, incunables, or incunes (books printed before 1501), than present-day concepts of printed books would seem to imply. While a modern book is radically different from a medieval manuscript, the first printers were not attempting to invent a new thing but trying to produce more expediently books looking as much as possible like those already familiar to their readers. The artwork in printed books was originally added by hand; later, woodcuts were used to facilitate the process by printing outlines that could be painted in by hand afterwards. What finally happened was the evolution of woodcut into an art form in its own right, which reached greatness in the sixteenth century, especially in the hands of Albrecht Dürer.

The use of carved stone, and of seals made from wood and other substances, to produce impressions on textiles or paper by rubbing or by stamping is very ancient, having been known in China and Japan in the first centuries A.D. Woodcut pictures circulated separately as charms before they were printed in books. The earliest woodcut picture in a printed book to which a definite date can be assigned occurs in a roll of Wang Chieh (868), containing the *Diamond Sutra,* now in the British Museum. The

◆§ Pictures and Decorations in Books

Diamond Sutra, like other printed books of the period, was produced from blocks containing units of text. The impressions were pasted together to form a scroll. The woodcut in question was printed from a separate block. The Chinese made block-books in which both pictures and text were produced from a single block long before this technique was known in Europe, and several centuries before their own craftsmen discovered movable type.[46]

In Europe, the printing of pictures from blocks was already a sophisticated art before the arrival of the printing press. Textile printing was known throughout the Middle Ages, and playing cards were printed from blocks at least as early as 1402.[47] Manuscripts, too, could have woodcut illustrations, as in HM 195 of the Huntington Library. One finds craftsmen cited under a variety of titles implying that they were engaged in some sort of printing, long before Gutenberg's successful venture into movable type for printing books.

The technical aspects of early block making and printing are not difficult to understand. The design was first conceived and drawn (or copied) by an artist, then drawn on the surface of the block. A woodcutter turned the drawing into a relief carving by paring away the surrounding surface. The blocks were made of fairly soft wood, such as pear, apple, cherry, sycamore, or beech, though boxwood, which had to be imported from Turkey, was favored in the late fifteenth century. There is evidence that some "woodcuts" of the time were actually printed from metal. Because of technical difficulties with the guilds over craft membership, it was usual for the artist and carver to be different individuals.

The ink was transferred to the material to receive print from the surface of the parts in relief, the rest appearing white when the impression was made. The ink had to be fairly thick and sticky for this purpose. Before the invention of the printing press, two methods of hand pressure were used: stamping, in which the inked block was laid face down on the material and pressed or hammered; and rubbing, in which the inked block was placed face up, the material laid over it and rubbed on the back with a hard object. Rubbing is found mostly in prints of the second and third quarters of the century, and the thinner ink used in their production to avoid smearing has tended to oxidize into brown.

Woodcut was first used by printers for pictures in their books *ca.* 1460-61, but not widely until 1467 in Italy and 1470 in Germany. This last date marks the beginning of the best period of woodcut art, which lasted until the end of the sixteenth century. As a book art, however, some authorities consider that, by Dürer's time, mass production had rendered the printers less careful of fine craftsmanship, regardless of the greater sophistication of the woodcuts themselves as works of art, and there is feeling that the best period of woodcut as book art, at least in Germany, was very brief: *ca.* 1470-1500. In Italy both Venice and Florence enjoyed periods of excellence in woodcut book illustration in the 1490s: the former for only that decade, the latter for somewhat longer. Florence excelled in a technique known as white line, in which the furrow, instead of the relief, becomes the line, the resulting print being in black with the design in white. Woodcut in England in the period under consideration in this study was black line.

Woodcut illustrations in the Chaucer incunabula are in all except name the work of William Caxton. Editions of the *Canterbury Tales* published by Richard Pynson (1492) and by Wynkyn de Worde (1498) contain Caxton's woodcuts or adaptations of them. It is well known that after bringing out an edition of the *Canterbury Tales* (*ca.* 1478), Caxton discovered that a better manuscript existed, and that he then printed a second edition, corrected from it (*ca.* 1484). It is this second edition which contains the series of twenty-three woodcuts of the pilgrims and the picture of the company gathered about a round table.[48] Nine copies of Caxton's second edition survive (ten of the first edition), the only perfect one in the Library of St. John's College, Oxford.

Of this perfect copy, Charles Muscatine notes that the woodcuts are "unfortunately" colored.[49] The misfortune is that present-day scholars should think the coloring of early woodcuts unfortunate. Woodcut artists intended their work to be painted, and understood their mission as providing the time-consuming outline

ৰ্ছ Pictures and Decorations in Books

drawing. Painted woodcut art in fifteenth-century books can be exquisitely beautiful, a true development of miniature painting, though this is not to deny that art so produced could fall into the hands of the unskilled, as indeed it often did, especially in this case. By Dürer's time, however, the public had become interested in woodcut as graphic art, and the typical occidental woodcut of the sixteenth century is not painted.

As for Caxton's woodcuts, the artist was no Dürer. They are by all standards crude, and it is not known whether Caxton made them himself or whether he employed someone for the purpose. More important, however, is the observation of William Blades that his early woodcuts were copied from the manuscripts from which he was working.[50] This, of course, raises the possibility that his second source-manuscript of the *Canterbury Tales* may have contained the originals of the now famous woodcuts. It should be noted that Caxton also made use of woodcut for initials in certain of his books and for the familiar printer's mark he began to use *ca.* 1488.

Both Richard Pynson and Wynkyn de Worde were foreigners, Pynson having been born in Normandy. He came to England in 1486, and his *Canterbury Tales* appeared in or before November 1492. Since there were no copyright laws or precedents to govern the professional rights of these first printers (who did not even have their own guild) there was nothing to prevent one from reissuing an earlier work or borrowing from it. Thus Pynson, who did not, so far as anyone knows, have access to Caxton's original blocks after the printer's death, made his own versions of the same woodcuts. De Worde, probably from Worth (in Alsace), is thought to have been Caxton's foreman.[51] He succeeded to Caxton's business when the printer died, *ca.* 1491, and his edition of the *Canterbury Tales* contains nineteen of the original woodcuts and two from Caxton's *The game and playe of the chesse*, presumably printed from Caxton's blocks.

In the sixteenth century, although books were still copied and illustrated by the old methods, printing began to dominate publishing, and the printed book became increasingly a thing apart from the hand-copied manuscript. If the year 1500 becomes an arbitrary date for concluding this discussion of artwork, it is true that, after this date, one enters upon the field of printing as a relatively modern technique, and woodcut becomes an art in its own right rather than a means of achieving more expediently the drawing necessary for hand-painted miniatures and other decoration proper to manuscripts.

It cannot be determined whether Chaucer had any of the works which were copied in his own lifetime supplied with artwork. He mentions his scribe by name, but says nothing about any artist in his employ. Even more fascinating is the question of the traditional likeness of the poet, for nothing is known about its origins except what can be deduced from Hoccleve's ambiguous comments in the *Regement of Princes*. Certainly the rank and file of Chaucer manuscripts contain no such elaborate artwork as the Ellesmere miniatures. One would do well to keep in mind that the run-of-the-mill medieval manuscript was a modest production which contained very little, if any, of the glorious artwork to which historians have to turn for the development of painting.

NOTES TO CHAPTER 2

[1] David Diringer, *The Illuminated Book*, rev. ed. (New York, 1967), p. 23.

[2] *The Book of the Art of Cennino Cennini*, trans. Christiana Jane (Powell) Herringham (London, 1899). See also Dino Formaggio and Carlo Basso, *A Book of Miniatures*, trans. Peggy Craig (London, 1962), pp. 50-76.

[3] For discussion, see below, pp. 37-38, 41-46.

[4] Authoritative historical works on English manuscript art are Eric George Millar, *English Illuminated Manuscripts from the Xth to the XIIIth Century* (Paris, 1926), and *English Illuminated Manuscripts of the XIVth and XVth Centuries* (Paris, 1928); Margaret Rickert, *Painting in Britain: The Middle Ages* (London, 1954). A more elementary and more general study is Jacques Dupont and Cesare Gnudi, *Gothic Painting* (Geneva, 1954). See also Formaggio and Basso, *A Book of Miniatures*.

[5] For earlier art in Britain, see Rickert, *Painting in Britain*, pp. 1-26; Plates 1-15.

‹§ Pictures and Decorations in Books

[6] Ibid., pp. 80-84; Plates 83-86. See also Walter Oakeshott, *The Artists of the Winchester Bible* (London, 1945).

[7] Montague Rhodes James, ed., *The Bestiary* (Oxford, 1928). See also Rickert, *Painting in Britain*, Plate 90.

[8] Beverly Boyd, *Chaucer and the Liturgy* (Philadelphia, 1968), pp. 65-67.

[9] *Early Netherlandish Painting* (Cambridge, Mass., 1953), I, 1-50.

[10] Rickert, *Painting in Britain*, pp. 129-30; Plates 129, 131. See also Sydney Carlyle Cockerell, ed., *The Gorleston Psalter* (London, 1907).

[11] Rickert, *Painting in Britain*, pp. 133-34; Plate 135. See also Eric George Millar, ed., *The Luttrell Psalter* (London, 1932).

[12] Rickert, *Painting in Britain*, pp. 127-28; Plates 127, 128. See also George Frederic Warner, ed., *Queen Mary's Psalter* (London, 1912).

[13] For an authoritative discussion of the International Style, see Panofsky, *Early Netherlandish Painting*, I, 51-74.

[14] Paul Durrieu, ed., *Les Très Riches Heures de Jean de France, Duc de Berry* (Paris, 1904).

[15] "A Giottesque Episode in English Mediaeval Art," *Journal of the Warburg and Courtauld Institutes*, 6 (1943), 51-70.

[16] *Liber Regalis*, ed. Frederick Lygon, 6th earl Beauchamp (London, 1870). For the miniature see *Painting in Britain*, p. 152; Plate 159.

[17] Rickert, *Painting in Britain*, pp. 157-60; Plates 160, 161. See also William George Constable, "The Date and Nationality of the Wilton Diptych," *The Burlington Magazine*, 55 (July-December, 1929), 36-45.

[18] Rickert, *Painting in Britain*, pp. 153-56; Plates 166, 167. See also Rickert, *The Reconstructed Carmelite Missal* (Chicago, 1952).

[19] Rickert, *Painting in Britain*, pp. 108-10; Plates 110-12. A useful reference work is Erardo Aeschlimann, *Dictionnaire des miniaturists du moyen age et de la renaissance* (Milan, 1940).

[20] Rickert, *Painting in Britain*, pp. 104-05; Plates 102, 103.

[21] Ibid., pp. 34-44; Plates 22, 23, 30.

[22] Ibid., pp. 163-65; Plates 164, 165. See also Millar, *Manuscripts of the XIVth and XVth Centuries*, Frontis., and John Alexander Herbert, ed., *The Sherborne Missal* (Oxford, 1920).

[23] Charles Louis Kuhn, "Herman Scheere and English Illumination of the Early Fifteenth Century," *The Art Bulletin*, 22 (1940), 138-56.

[24] Rickert, *Painting in Britain*, pp. 165-71; Plates 169-76. For the Brussels MS., see P. Pintelon, ed., *Chaucer's Treatise on the Astrolabe* (Antwerp, 1940).

[25] "Illumination," in M-R, I, 561-605.

[26] *The Portraits of Geoffrey Chaucer*, Chaucer Society, 2nd Ser., No. 31 (London, 1900).

[27] For color reproductions, see *The Ellesmere Chaucer Reproduced in Facsimile* (Manchester, 1911). See also Herbert C. Schulz, *The Ellesmere Manuscript of Chaucer's "Canterbury Tales"* (San Marino, Calif., 1966); the manuscript is described by M-R, I, 148-59.

[28] Schulz, *Ellesmere Manuscript*, pp. 3-4.

[29] The portraits in Gg are reproduced by Frederick James Furnivall, ed., *Autotypes of Chaucer Manuscripts*, Chaucer Society, 1st Ser., Nos. 48, 56, 62, 74 (published loose in portfolio, London, 1876-86); No. 56, pp. 3-14. See also Margaret Rickert, "Illumination," M-R, I, 590-604; Roger Sherman Loomis, *A Mirror of Chaucer's World* (Princeton, 1965), p. 80.

[30] M-R, I, 396-98.

[31] Ibid., I, 198-206.

[32] Reproduced by Furnivall, *Autotypes*, No. 56, pp. 15-20.

[33] *The Complete Works of John Gower*, ed. George Campbell Macaulay, I, *The French Works* (Oxford, 1899), 13-14.

[34] M-R, I, 596-97.

[35] Ibid., 597-98.

[36] For text with portrait, see Spielmann, *Portraits of Chaucer*, p. 7. See also Frederick James Furnivall, ed., *Hoccleve's Works*, EETS, Extra Ser., Nos. 61 (London, 1892), 72 (1897), 73 (1925: ed. Israel Gollancz). *The Regement of Princes* is in the second volume.

[37] Spielmann, *Portraits of Chaucer*, p. 9.

[38] "The Early English School of Portraiture," *The Burlington Magazine*, 65 (July-December, 1934), 175.

[39] Ibid., pp. 171-75.

[40] *Chaucer's Poetry* (New York, 1958), pp. 877-81.

[41] For color reproduction, see Dupont and Gnudi, *Gothic Painting*, p. 164. See also Margaret Galway, "The 'Troilus' Frontispiece," *MLR*, 44 (1949), 161-77. This article seeks to establish identities for the people in the miniature.

ۍ *Pictures and Decorations in Books*

[42]Spielmann, p. 11; M-R, I, 584-87; 64-70; 117-21.

[43]M-R, I, 564.

[44]M-R, I, 565-81; all manuscripts listed are described by M-R.

[45]For a complete study of woodcut, see Arthur Mayger Hind, *An Introduction to a History of Woodcut* (Boston, 1935).

[46]The authoritative work on the history of oriental printing is Thomas Francis Carter, *The Invention of Printing in China and Its Spread Westward* (2nd ed., rev. L. Carrington Goodrich, New York, 1955).

[47]Hind, *Introduction to a History of Woodcut*, pp. 67ff.

[48]See below, p. 127, and Plates XI and XII.

[49]*The Book of Geoffrey Chaucer* (San Francisco, 1963), p. 8.

[50]*The Life and Typography of William Caxton* (London, 1861-63), II, liv.

[51]Henry Robert Plomer, *Wynkyn de Worde & His Contemporaries* (London, 1925).

3

Writing in Books

IF CHAUCER says nothing about employing an artist, he does indeed specify that he employed someone to put his drafts into manuscript. Today he would have engaged a typist, no doubt with the same complaint he wrote in lines addressed to one Adam:

> Adam scriveyn, if ever it thee bifalle
> Boece or Troylus for to wryten newe,
> Under thy long lokkes thou most have the scalle,
> But after my makyng thou wryte more trewe;
> So ofte a-daye I mot thy werk renewe,
> It to correcte and eek to rubbe and scrape;
> And al is thorugh thy negligence and rape.

This Adam, it seems, made mistakes as he transcribed, which put Chaucer to the trouble of correcting his copy. The scribe is now an extinct species. But he was the most important agent in book production, next to the author himself, until the printer-editor appeared upon the scene in the fifteenth century.

For the most part the medieval scribe is anonymous. Outside the religious orders he worked long hours for no great reward in a society which set little economic value upon the skills of literacy, however much it prized books. To his heirs of a later day, however, the scribe is very much more important, for scholars working with manuscripts are at his mercy. There is often nothing but his word that an author meant what he, the scribe, says he meant. Over some of the most significant lines in medieval poetry broods the shadow of possible scribal error. Indeed, a popular saying

Writing in Books

among medievalists (probably untrue) is that a dull scribe was the most reliable practitioner of his art, since he was least likely to tamper with his text. Chaucer's Adam, however, may not have been so stupid—or there would have been no point in writing him a witty poem.

Here some definitions are necessary. The study of old handwriting is known as "paleography."[1] Paleography is a scholar's term which, in the strictest sense, applies only to handwriting itself. But since it is impossible to study old handwriting in abstraction from its milieu, discussion of paleography necessarily includes adjunct topics pertaining to manuscripts, some of which have already been covered in connection with binding and illumination. A more general term referring to the art of penmanship, ancient or modern, is "calligraphy." Also, any kind of handwriting can be called a "script."

The professional scriptorium was a simple operation. The scribe needed only a table with a lectern or sloping top, good light, a stand for his original copy, writing material, pen, ink, a knife for cutting his quills, and pumice for erasing and for adjusting the surface of his parchment. He also needed a stylus of some sort for pricking his margins and for ruling. In the later Middle Ages a plummet was used for ruling. This general situation, familiar to the Greeks and Romans (who, however, used reed pens for writing on papyrus), became the basis of monastic publishing.

Under the Rule of St. Benedict the work of copying books, as well as the reading of them, prospered through the philosophy that idleness is bad for the soul.[2] The monks were required to work, and the labor of the scriptorium was part of the daily routine through which the monastery managed to be as self-sufficient as possible. Aside from the fact that the monastic scriptorium bestowed riches upon western civilization, the monastic environment placed the control of books and their contents solidly in the hands of the Church, where it remained until the rise of the universities in the eleventh and twelfth centuries.

The copying of a book was ordinarily, and ideally, done by one man, one page at a time. The process could be speeded by removing the original from its binding and dealing out the gatherings to several scribes, who could then work simultaneously upon the same volume. The drawbacks to this system were the inevitable differences in handwriting among the sections of the finished book. Many books were done this way, however, and it is common to find more than one handwriting. Of course there could be other factors involved, such as the death or unavailability of the original scribe.

All writing in western Europe came sooner or later to employ the Roman alphabet, basically the same as that now used for writing English except that it had no *w*, and that it did not distinguish between the forms *i-j* or *u-v*. Words were not ordinarily separated from each other in Classical Latin, ambiguity being avoided either by separation or by use of a *punctum* or 'point.'[3] While most Classical Latin literature survives in early medieval copies, the Romans themselves wrote their books in capitals, or majuscules. There were two basic styles of capitals: square capitals, still familiar in monument inscriptions, and rustic capitals, so named by paleographers because the writing shows greater freedom. Among other features, horizontals on the right may project to the left of the verticals, giving a less rigid appearance. The Romans were writing their books in rustic capitals in the first century A.D. By the fifth century books were being written in a more rounded majuscule known as "uncial" (Lat. *uncialis* 'inch-high'). Western European books from the fifth century to the eighth are chiefly in this clear and handsome script.[4]

In dealing with handwriting used for books it must be understood that other, less laborious scripts known as "cursives" and characterized by joined letters, have always prevailed for ordinary uses. Unlike the cursives used earlier for writing Latin, which had been made up of straight strokes, western European cursives after about the fourth century were formed of curves.[5] The kinds of writing used at various times and in various places for documents rather than for books, and therefore traditionally known as "court" or "charter" hands, were cursives. In the later Middle Ages cursive influences came to dominate book hands, and even-

◆§ *Writing in Books*

tually replaced them.⁶ Practical writing habits are thus seen to be partly responsible for the changing styles of book hands through the centuries.

Returning to the uncial script, a modified form of it came into use as a book hand in Italy and in southern France. Still a majuscule script, although it had ascenders and descenders projecting above and below the line of writing, it admitted increasingly cursive influences in the form of letters that were more rounded, and it could therefore be written more comfortably and more quickly. Known to paleographers as "half-uncial," although Stanley Morison considers "half-minuscule" more appropriate, it was prominent in copying by the sixth century.⁷ The script was taken to Ireland, probably from the monastic schools of southern France—if not (as tradition has it) by St. Patrick himself, certainly by missionaries of the saint's period or shortly thereafter. In Ireland it developed into a national hand during the relative isolation which came to that part of the world after the fall of Rome. The most famous example of the Irish half-uncial is the Books of Kells.⁸ The half-uncial went with the Irish monks to their missionary foundations in England and to places as far away as Switzerland and northern Italy. With slight modification of style, it is the script of the Lindisfarne Gospels, the handwriting of this famous book differing from that of the Book of Kells chiefly in being clearer and more stout.⁹

During this period smaller and more rapid book hands were developing all over Europe. These hands, some of them very difficult to read, are known as "minuscule" writing. Minuscule letters are what would now be called small, or lower case, letters, in contrast with majuscules, or capitals. Minuscule scripts were easier and faster to produce and, more important in view of the expense and shortage of parchment, reduced production costs by requiring less parchment. But minuscule letters are not merely smaller letters than majuscules, since either could be written in any desired size. Their formation is different, being much more rounded than majuscule writing, and having, like half-uncial, a four-line principle of construction, with the vertical stems of elongated letters rising or falling well above or below the line of writing.

The Irish developed their own form of minuscule writing, as did the Anglo-Saxons, who achieved a rather pointed style.[10] Since they used this script for their vernacular literature, the Anglo-Saxons added to it symbols for sounds not represented by the Roman alphabet. These symbols, of runic origin, are ƿ: "wynn," w; þ: "thorn," th; and ð: "eth," also th.[11] Since this writing is not indigenously English, it cannot be called either native or English when discussed in comparison with other handwriting, and it is called instead "Insular."[12]

Of the minuscule hands, the most important historically is that known as Caroline or Carolingian minuscule[13] which developed in the Frankish kingdom. Based on half-uncial, this minuscule differs from others especially in the fact that it was carefully freed from certain cursive elements present in its evolution. The individual letters are isolated, carefully aligned, and elegantly formed, giving simplicity and clarity to the written page. Its objective was discipline, not speed or ease in writing.

In England the Insular hand persisted until the Norman Conquest, influenced by the Caroline minuscule but not replaced by it. It became customary to use the Caroline script for works written in Latin and the Insular hand for works in the vernacular, a situation not directly changed by the Conquest except that the Insular hand was reserved for the English vernacular. An exchange of influences, however, was inevitable, and by the twelfth century the Insular hand had disappeared except for the symbols derived from the runic alphabet.

The Insular g, however, which was written ȝ and which is called *yogh*, was carried into the Caroline minuscule script. Until the end of the Middle English period it was used in addition to the Caroline minuscule g to represent certain sounds peculiar to the English vernacular. The voiced velar stopped consonant was spelled g (i.e., *gon, game*), but *yogh* was used as a palatal and velar spirant (i.e., *ȝer, riȝt*). After about 1300, this *yogh* began to be replaced initially by y, and elsewhere by gh or h (i.e., *right, riht*). Editors preparing normalized texts use *gh* or *h* for *yogh* in this situation, depending upon the scribe's own consistency. Obviously, if he sometimes writes one of these spellings the editor will prefer the scribe's own usage in the matter—unless he has the misfortune to be dealing with a scribe who has more than one!

It should also be noted that in the Northwest Midland dialect of Middle English *yogh* was used at the ends of words with the phonetic value of *z* or *s*. In normalizing, editors usually write this *yogh* as *z*. In Scots *yogh* was often spelled *ʒh*. It should be noted further that þ gradually replaced ð for the sound now spelled *th*, and that þ was, by the time of the Chaucer manuscripts, more a scribal abbreviation than a letter of the alphabet. Indeed, scribes sometimes wrote both þ and *th*, and they used the form þ^e, "the," in manuscripts where they regularly used the spelling *th* instead of þ. *Wynn* had also disappeared by that time, being replaced by *u*, *uu*, and *w*, this last symbol having been introduced by Norman scribes in the twelfth century.

The Caroline minuscule, like other scripts, began to acquire regional characteristics once it had come into wide use. Of more immediate concern are the reflections in handwriting of the major trends in art: first, the Romanesque, which matched large, splendid volumes with large script notable for clarity and for such perfection in form that the twelfth century is widely held to be the best period of minuscule book hand;[14] second, the Gothic, in which book hand moved, like other manuscript art, toward the small size and elegance typical of the thirteenth century. This was produced, among other factors, by maintaining exactness in letter formation while achieving lateral compression through substitution of angular lines for curves and also through closer placement of verticals. These features give the writing a pointed, angular appearance, and the script itself has become known, for that reason, as Gothic, although that term was not used at the time (Plate IV).[15]

An important adjunct to Gothic writing was an increasing reliance upon one of the most important scribal techniques, abbreviation. While abbreviation had always been part of the scribe's procedure, it was now more heavily used than before, an attribute which makes Gothic writing rather cryptic and much more difficult to read than the best handwriting of the twelfth century. Abbreviation is, in general, so basic to medieval manuscripts of all periods that it is impossible to read them without some knowledge of the principles involved.

The word "abbreviation" is a poor term for the subject since more is involved than mere word shortening. There are four basic principles, originally devised for writing Greek and Latin and eventually adapted to the writing of western European vernaculars, including English:

1. Suspension, or omission of final letters of the word, shown either by a dot (e.g. *R.* for *Rex*) or by a horizontal line above the last letter written (e.g., *hostē*, for *hostem*).
2. Contraction, or omission of medial letters, shown by a horizontal line above the word (e.g., *dn̄s*, for *dominus*, *ap̄ti* for *apostoli*).
3. The use of superior letters (e.g., $q^a m$, for *quam*).
4. The use of special signs.[16]

The fourth category is the most difficult to deal with, because it concerns, not a method, but a vocabulary of scribal abbreviations, often involved in Latin inflections, and in some cases used in a wide and ambiguous range of applications.[17] Perhaps the most interesting of these historically are certain symbols derived from a system of shorthand associated with Cicero's freedman, Tiro, and therefore called Tironian notes. Examples are 7, for *et*, and 9, for the prefix (and preposition) *cum* and its variants *cun*, *con*, *com* (e.g., *cir9scriptum*, for *circumscriptum*).

To this fourth category also belongs a variety of meaningful strokes through other letters, such as: an oblique stroke through tall letters, especially through *l*, a general sign of contraction or suspension; a waved vertical stroke, sometimes written as a curve rising from the preceding letter, a sign of the omission of *er* or *re*; a long drooping stroke at the end of a word, a sign for the omis-

◆§ *Writing in Books*

sion of any termination. The letter *p* was especially subject to signs of abbreviation: a curve through the stem indicating *pro*; a horizontal bar through the stem indicating *per, par, por*; a horizontal or waved stroke or curve above it (in nonterminal positions) indicating *pre*. One of the most troublesome signs in fifteenth-century English vernacular manuscripts is a reflex curve on *r* at the end of a word, which traditionally indicated a final *e*, but which often became confused with flourishes in the scribal handwriting. Sometimes the rhymes are the only evidence of the correct reading.

Gothic script might show considerable differences in the degree of formality with which it was written. The most calligraphic writing the scribes could produce was used for liturgical books, while other books might be written more freely and more rapidly in script which was still Gothic. Thus, there were "hierarchies" of scripts. But Gothic was impractical for many reasons, and, in the second half of the thirteenth century, books copied in English scriptoria, other than liturgical books, were increasingly written in cursive scripts. M. B. Parkes explains this development, not merely as a movement away from the rigidity of Gothic, but also as a practical answer to an increasing demand for books, about which more will be said later.[18] Chaucer's scribe Adam undoubtedly wrote in one of these cursive hands when he copied *Boece* and *Troilus*.

To understand these cursive book hands, it is necessary to know what is meant by the term "duct": the manner in which pen and hand were positioned and maneuvered while approaching and using the parchment or paper. In cursive writing, the scribe employed curved strokes in preference to straight ones. Also, he handled his pen so that it left the writing surface as seldom as possible. He produced on that account connecting strokes, not only between letters but between parts of the same letter, these connecting strokes becoming auxiliary characteristics of the letters themselves.[19]

In the fourteenth and fifteenth centuries, there were two general varieties of English cursive book hands, Anglicana and Secretary. Anglicana is the earlier, recognizable in manuscripts of the second half of the thirteenth century. Its chief characteristics, even this soon, are as follows: *a* having two compartments, the upper one being large and extending above the general height of the letter; *d* having a looped ascender; *f* and long *s* having long descenders, curving to the left below the line of writing and frequently followed by a connecting stroke to the top of the letter; *g* having two compartments in the manner of a figure 8; *r* having a long stem; short *s* having a form based on that of the capital. These and other features of the new script passed through several modifications, including, in the late thirteenth century, elaboration of the ascenders of *b*, *h*, *k*, and *l* into forked effects.

In the early part of the fourteenth century this writing was greatly revised. The forked ascenders disappeared and approach strokes developed to the right of the ascenders, either into a flat loop or into a hook. A new cursive *e* made its appearance, the stem and lobe being formed in a single circular movement. The letter *h* acquired a descender below the line of writing, and the letter *r* acquired a more pronounced connecting stroke between the descender and the shoulder, the shoulder itself eventually disappearing. The duct was also modified, the angle of the pen being changed from oblique to almost upright, giving a more vertical appearance to the writing. What emerged was a rapid, clear script, useful not only for documents but for inexpensive books. Paleographers before Parkes have usually called this writing "court" or "charter" hand, but the name Anglicana is more realistic when referring to its use in books as well as in documents, and because of its English origin.

Anglicana lacked the calligraphic qualities which had distinguished liturgical hands and highly formal book hands from other Gothic writing. But this kind of formal writing, often called "Textura," was becoming merely imitative, and there was a movement toward larger, more calligraphic, Anglicana script for finer books. Scribes addressed themselves to more meticulous formation of letters, a characteristic most easily seen in the letter *m*, each minim (short, vertical stroke) being produced with a separate

ঽ Writing in Books

stroke, finished with a foot, instead of with a single, connected one. The letters were made larger and, as a result, the letters *a* and short *s* no longer extended so far above the level of the other writing, and in most cases the ascenders and descenders of the other letters were proportionately shorter than those of less formal Anglicana script. In addition, certain characteristic forms appeared: *d* with its looped ascender having a more upright, or even straight, back; *t* with a shaft extended farther above the headstroke; short s having a capital form; the short form of *r* sometimes appearing. Parkes calls this more calligraphic and more formal Anglicana script "Anglicana Formata." Anglicana Formata is the major book hand of fourteenth-century English scribes. At the very end of that century and in the early fifteenth, it was used for some large manuscripts containing vernacular literature. Notable among these is the Ellesmere Chaucer (Plate VII).

An even more formal handwriting was developed for display purposes (titles, colophons, and the like) as well as for books. This was achieved by blending a larger version of Anglicana Formata with Gothic, the result being what Parkes calls "Bastard Anglicana." The term "bastard" is used in the study of handwriting to describe a union between a baser script and a more calligraphic one. Bastard Anglicana can be found in manuscripts of the mid-fourteenth century and later.[20]

The second major type of cursive book hand used in English scriptoria in the later Middle Ages is called "Secretary." It is thought to have originated in Italy. From there it spread to France where it developed before making its appearance in English books toward the end of the fourteenth century (Plate VIII). While most of the basic strokes are the same as in Anglicana, the duct is different, and angular, broken strokes appear where curved strokes are more usual, especially in the lobes of *a, d, g*; in the formation of *o*; in a *z*-shaped *r*; and in the formation of *c* and *e*. A forked effect appears on the tops of letters, especially *e, g, t,* and short *s*. The descenders of *f*, long *s*, and *p* are exaggerated. Finally, English Secretary script has forms of *a, g, r,* and short *s* which do not appear in other contemporary English writing. Throughout

Chaucer and the Medieval Book 🙵

PLATE VII (Anglicana Formata)

Features: two-compartment *a*; long *r*; 8-shaped *g*; *h* with long descender; *m*, *n* with separate-stroke minims, with feet; *d* with looped ascender; short *s* based on capital form. But note occasional *z*-shaped *r*. Capitalization regular at beginnings of lines, not elsewhere. Occasional use of *þ*, but the scribe normally uses *th*. The meaning of the light slash appearing in most lines is unclear.

    Whan that Aprill with hise shoures soote
    The droghte of March hath perced to the roote
    And bathed euery veyne in swich licour
    Of which ve*r*tu engendred is the flour
5 Whan Zephirus eek w*ith* his sweete breeth
    Inspired hath in euery holt and heeth
    The tendre croppes and the yonge sonne
    Hath in the Ram his half cours yronne   ¶ 1. sol in ariet
    And smale foweles maken melodye
10 That slepen al the nyght with open eye
    So priketh hem nature in hir corages
    Thanne longen folk to goon on pilg*r*image*s*
    And Palme*r*es for to seken straunge strondes
    To ferne halwes kowthe in sondry londes
15 And specially fram euery shires ende
    Of Engelond to Caunt*er*bury they wende
    The hooly blissful martir for to seke
    That hem hath holpen whan *that* they were seeke
    Bifil that in that seson on a day
20 In Southwerk at the Tabard as I lay
    Redy to wenden on my pilgrymage
    To Caunt*er*bury with ful deuout corage

Notes: 1 Scribes often exaggerated ascenders in a first line. *With:* cf. *w*^{t}, line 5.

Aprill: the bar through double *l* is still taken by some scholars to mean-*lle*, which would be normal in Latin manuscripts. While the line reads well either way, the best evidence indicates that the form *-lle* is unlikely in view of the later history of the word in English.

3 The scribe regularly dots *y*.

68

Writing in Books

PLATE VII. An example of Anglicana Formata bookhand from the Ellesmere Manuscript of the *Canterbury Tales*

Chaucer and the Medieval Book

PLATE VIII (Secretary)

Features: headless *a*; *r* either short or *z*-shaped; *g* with long descender; descenders exaggerated and tapered, sloping to the left; capitalization inconsistent; small loops on ascenders; long and short forms of *s*.

20 It was me tolde er ye come here two oures
he was parde an olde felaw of youres
Al sodeynly was he slayne to night
ffordronken as he sat vpon his benche vpright
ther come a prive theef men clepe deth
25 that in his cuntre all peple sleeth
And with his spere he smote his herte atwo
And went his way withoute wordes moo
he hath a thousand slayn this pestilence
And maister er ye come in presence
30 Me thynkith it were necessary
fforto be war of soche an aduersary
Beth redi forto mete hym evir more
thus taught me my dame I say no more
Be seynt mary saide this tavernere
35 the childe saith sothe for he hathe slayn to yere
hennes ouer a myle within a grete village
Bothe man and woman childe and page
I trow his habitacion be there
to be avised grete wisdom it were
40 Or that he did a man dishonoure
Ye goddes armes quod this riatoure
Is it soche peril with hym forto mete
I shal hym seche be sty and be strete
I make a vow be the digne goddes bones

Notes: 34-35: The scribe mixes final *r* + *e* with final *r* looped for abbreviated final *e*; throughout, he shows a confusing tendency to loop final *r* whether or not final *e* is intended.

Writing in Books

> It was me tolde er ye come here two oures
> he was parde an olde felaw of youres
> Al sodeynly was he slayne to nyght
> ffordronken as he sat vpon his benche vpright
> ther come a priue theef men clepe deth
> that in his contree al peple sleeth
> And with his spere he smote his herte atwo
> And went his way withoute wordes mo
> he hath a thousand slayn this pestilence
> And master er ye come in presence
> Me thynkith it were necessary
> fforto be war of soche an aduersary
> Beth redy forto mete hym eūmore
> thus taught me my dame I say no more
> Be seynt mary sayde this tauerner
> the childe seith sothe for he hath slayn to yere
> hennes ouer a myle within a grete villane
> Bothe man and woman childe and page
> I trow his habitacion be there
> to be aduysed grete wysdome it were
> Or that he did a man dishonour
> ye goddes armes quod this riotour
> Is it soche peril with hym forto mete
> I shal hym seche be sty and be strete
> I make avow be the diuine goddes bones

PLATE VIII. An example of Secretary bookhand from a fifteenth-century manuscript

Chaucer and the Medieval Book

PLATE IX (Anglicana Formata with Secretary forms)

Features: frequent broken strokes instead of curves; *r* short or z-shaped; horned ascenders; *a* headless or two-compartment; use of þ and *th*; *d* with straight back, looped ascender; *g* with long descender, curving to the left; capitalization regular at beginnings of lines; *w* exaggerated.

    The double sorwe of Troylus to tellen.
    That was þe kyng Priamus sone of Troye.
    In louynge how his auentures fellen.
    ffro wo to wele and after out of Joye.
5   My purpos is er þat I parte froye.
    Thesiphone þow helpe me for tendite.
    These woful vers. þat wepen as I write.
    To þe clepe I þow goddesse of torment.
    Thow cruel furie sorwyng euere yn peyne.
10 Help me that am the sorwful Instrument.
    That helpeth louers as I kan to pleyne.
    ffor wel sit it the sothe for to seyne.
    A woful wight to han a drery feere.
    And to a sorwful tale a sory cheere.
15 For I þat god of loues seruauntz serue.
    Ne dar to loue for myn vnliklynesse.
    Preyen for sped al shold .I. þerfor sterue.
    So fer am fro his help in derknesse.
    But natheles if þis may don gladnesse.
20 Un to ony louere and his cause auayle.
    Haue he my þank and myn be his trauayle.

Notes: The handwriting becomes less careful as the scribe passes the middle of the page. The reason for points at the ends of lines is uncertain; the scribe uses a point as a comma, line 30.

    4 *froye:* perhaps a scribal error, but the form should be written together for rime.

    6 *tendite:* There is no apostrophe this early; such forms are common results of elision.

≼§ *Writing in Books*

PLATE IX. An example of Anglicana Formata with Secretary forms from the early fifteenth-century Campsall Manuscript

Chaucer and the Medieval Book

PLATE X. Caxton's Type No. 2

Features: type based on Bastard Secretary handwriting of Flanders. Flourishes on terminal *d* and *g* not to be confused with scribal abbreviations. Capitalization regular at beginnings of lines, but elsewhere irregular. Initials added by hand.

Kepe bettir thy good this gyue I in charge
Thus endith my tale and god vs sende
Talyng ynough vnto our lyuys ende
  Here endith the Shipmannys tale+
   Verba Hospitis+
WEl said by corpus *dominus* sayde our ost
Now longe moot thou sayle by the cost
Thou gentil maister gentil mariner

PLATE XI. Caxton's Type No. 4*

Features: smaller than Type No. 2. Final *d* and *g* have flourishes, not to be confused with scribal abbreviations.

   Prologue
GRet chere made our ost to vs euerychon
And to soupere sette he vs anon
He serued vs wyth vytayll at the beste
Strong was the wyne *and* wel drynke vs lyste
A semely man our oste was wyth alle
Forto be a marchal in a lordes halle
A large man he was with eyen stepe

Note: The signature appears in the bottom margin, close to the text. The title is in Type No. 2*.

Writing in Books

> Kepe bettir thy goodꝛ this gyue I in charge
> Thus endith my tale andꝛ godꝛ vs sende
> Talyngꝛ ynough vnto our lyues ende
>   Here endith the Shipmannys tale.
>   Verba Hospitis.
> Wel saidꝛ by corpus dñs sayde our ost
> Moſt longe moot thou sayle by the cost
> Thou gentil maiſter gentil mariner

PLATE X. An example of Caxton's Type No. 2, from his first edition of the *Canterbury Tales*

> Ret chere made our oſt to vs euerychon
> Andꝛ to souper sette he vs anon
> He serued vs wyth vytayll at the beſte
> Stronge was the wyne ⁊ wel dꝛynke vs lyſte
> A semely man our oſte was wyth alle
> Forto be a marchal in a lordes halle
> A large man he was wyth eyen ſtepe

PLATE XI. An example of Caxton's Type No. 4*, from his second edition of the *Canterbury Tales*

75

the fifteenth century, Secretary script becomes increasingly common in English books and documents.[21]

Secretary script, like Anglicana, developed bastard forms in the fifteenth century, but under somewhat different circumstances, for Secretary, being also used on the Continent, developed regional characteristics there. The first printer to work in English, William Caxton, not only learned printing on the Continent, but did his earliest work in Belgium, where he acquired his types. The models for these, since there were no precedents for type other than contemporary handwriting, were a form of Secretary handwriting then used in Flanders, where the types were cast, and therefore known as Flemish Bâtarde. This is very important, for comparison of Plates X and XI with other plates showing contemporary handwriting will make clear the fact that there is little difference, other than mechanical process, between late medieval manuscripts and incunabula.

An essay of this kind necessarily oversimplifies the true state of things in order to emphasize major developments. Anglicana did not abruptly cease to exist with the entrance of Secretary script into the English ateliers. Instead, scribes writing in Anglicana did so under the influence of the new script, the first major impact being the use of broken strokes instead of curves. In manuscripts written at the beginning of the fifteenth century this characteristic is quite pronounced, as is the presence of horn-like tops on certain letters, notably *e, g, t,* and short *s*. These features made certain of the Anglicana letters difficult to write and the scribes devised easier methods of producing them which somewhat altered the forms. The incidence of simplified forms in the Anglicana script increases during the fifteenth century. By the second half, the scribes were so accustomed to Secretary that their writing habits carried over, making the writing of Anglicana less disciplined and more mixed with Secretary forms.

Anglicana Formata and Bastard Anglicana, being meticulously written, show the influence of the new script early and clearly. Broken strokes tend to appear in the lobes of *d* and *g* during the last quarter of the fourteenth century, and shortly thereafter in

Writing in Books

the formation of other letters, especially *a, c, g,* and *o,* as well as in the loops of some ascenders. The short *r* derived from earlier book hands was remodeled by analogy with the Secretary form. The outstanding examples of Anglicana Formata belong to about 1400, when a number of large vernacular books were produced in that hand. It was the standard hand for at least fifty years, when scribes began to replace it with Bastard Secretary. After that, of course, the advent of printing gave an entirely new direction to the production of books in Europe.

The best way to learn to read manuscripts is by studying plates against transcriptions. References have been given to appropriate sources. The few representative plates that can be given here have been selected from the Chaucer manuscripts, with the exception of Plate IV, which is from a psalter and illustrates Gothic liturgical hand.[22]

Although scribes usually did their work exceedingly well, anyone copying from an exemplar for hours at a time was bound to make occasional mistakes. The subject of scribal error is very important, not only because it often accounts for difficulties in a text but because any variation in readings among manuscripts means that someone, the editor, must eventually decide which is the correct, or at least the best, reading.

When a mistake occurred in the process of copying, it could be erased by scraping with a knife or by rubbing with pumice—methods Chaucer obviously used on the lapses made by the scribe Adam. Mistakes could also be stroked out, or canceled by underdotting. Extensive errors could be canceled by writing in an appropriate place the word *vacat,* or the whole leaf could be cut out. Scribes attempted to do their corrections in ways that did not interfere with the appearance of their work. Unhappily for their successors, their mistakes sometimes went undetected or, even worse, ignored. It is not uncommon, moreover, for manuscripts to contain corrections made by a later hand.

The topic of scribal error is a large one, and only a few of the most common types can be discussed here. These will be illustrated by examples from the *Canterbury Tales.* Since Manly and

Rickert have printed the corpus of variant readings, lists of manuscripts will not be given. In studying the examples, it is necessary to know that the editor (Robinson) has used modern English punctuation and capitalization, and that he has normalized *u* and *v*. In editing a text, there are other options, such as more extensive normalization, or diplomatic editing. The second method follows the manuscripts literally.

Particularly common among scribal errors are eye-skips. In the Physician's tale (VI, 283-84), the narrator says, "For be he lewed man, or ellis lered, / He noot how soone that he shal been afered." The scribe of the Hengwrt Manuscript accidentally omitted *he* in line 283, and added it above the line.[23] An eye-skip could also cause the scribe to leave out a line or an entire passage. In MS. Harley 7334 of the British Museum (*ca.* 1410), the scribe omitted from the Second Nun's tale seven lines (VIII,210-16). The circumstances are not difficult to identify. The passage, and the lines immediately before and after, should read,

> Aboven alle and over alle everywhere."
> Thise wordes al with gold ywriten were.
>
> Whan this was rad, thanne seyde this olde man,
> "Leevestow this thyng or no? Sey ye or nay."
> "I leeve al this thyng," quod Valerian,
> "For sother thyng than this, I dar wel say,
> Under the hevene no wight thynke may."
> Tho vanysshed the olde man, he nyste where,
> And Pope Urban hym cristned right there.   (ll. 209-17)

The scribe, however, skipped from *everywhere,* at the end of line 209, to *where,* which occupies the same position in line 216. Coincidentally, he thereby appeared to have finished a stanza.[24] Similar errors are also common in prose. There are many in the Parson's tale throughout the Chaucer manuscripts.

The scribe's memory, as well as his eyes, could play tricks upon him. This is the case in a passage of the Man of Law's tale (II, 981-87), as it appears in MS. Gg.4.27 (1420-40) of Cambridge University. The scribe copied these lines—an entire stanza—and then, forgetting that he had done so, proceeded to repeat them. The error is marked *vacat*.[25] Errors of memory are especially common in lines of verse involving lists. Having read his line, the scribe might set down the items in reverse order, or even garble them. A classic example occurs in the Knight's tale (I, 2949), where Chaucer describes the libations poured upon Arcite's funeral pyre. The Ellesmere scribe wrote the line as follows (without, of course, the modern editor's punctuation):

> And coppes fulle of wyn, and milk, and blood.

Numerous variants appear in other manuscripts, in different spellings: *milk and wyn*; *wyn milk*; *wyn*; *weyn of milk*; *milk weyn*.[26] In another kind of memory lapse, the scribe might repeat something he had just written in the previous line. Indeed, if he had copied works by Chaucer before, he might unconsciously write a variant reading he happened to remember, instead of what was in his exemplar.

The sounds of language could also cause confusion. In the Second Nun's Prologue (VIII, 89-91), the Ellesmere scribe wrote,

> Or, for she whitnesse hadde of honestee,
> And grene of conscience, and of good fame
> The soote savour, "lilie" was hir name.

The word *whitnesse* certainly refers to the whiteness of the lily, contrasted with its *grene* in the next line. But a few manuscripts have instead *witnesse*, obviously the spelling of some scribe accustomed to vocalize initial *w* in the combination *wh*, whose manuscript had been used as an exemplar.[27] Similarly, a scribe might lapse into his own dialect for a word or two. Occasional slips of dialect are frequent in Middle English manuscripts, and those containing works by Chaucer have their share. On a larger scale, the scribe John Duxworth put a manuscript of the *Canterbury Tales* into his own Northern dialect: MS. Fonds Anglais 39 (*ante* 1430) of the Bibliothèque Nationale (Paris). The book was made for the French political prisoner John of Angoulême (brother of the poet Charles of Orléans), who must have preferred English in Northern dialect since he supervised the copying himself.[28]

The scribe might make other mistakes in dealing with such problems as difficult handwriting, abbreviations which were ambiguous or carelessly written, or unfamiliar words. A case involving difficulties in the handwriting of some early exemplar may be found in the Knight's tale. In the Ellesmere and Hengwrt manuscripts, and in five others, I, 2713-14 reads as follows:

> Fermacies of herbes, and eek save
> They dronken, for they wolde hir lymes have.

But all other manuscripts read *lyves*, or *lyve*, not *lymes*. The word *lyves*, of course, appears in the manuscripts written *lyues*, and it is virtually impossible to distinguish *u* from other letters composed of minims in certain contexts. One of these readings must be correct, but which? Although *lyves* seems to make better sense, editors accept the agreement of Ellesmere and Hengwrt as authority for *lymes*.[29] The authority of these two manuscripts in matters of text will be discussed shortly.[30]

With regard to abbreviations, the most troublesome in Middle English manuscripts is the reflex curve on *r* at the end of a word, which traditionally meant *re*. But the unstressed final *e* was ceasing to be pronounced, and the scribes often mistook it for a flourish in the handwriting of their exemplar, even in cases where the abbreviation occurred as an intended rhyme with a word having the *e* written out. The difficulties involved in dealing with this abbreviation may be seen in Plate VIII.

An abbreviation could also cause trouble inside a word. In the Knight's tale (I, 2037), Robinson's edition reads,

> As is depeynted in the sterres above

But the Ellesmere scribe wrote *sertres*, not *sterres*, and Robinson has corrected the line from manuscripts that have the word Chaucer obviously intended to write. Manly and Rickert believe that the exemplar which led to the original error contained the letters *stres*, and that there was a carelessly written abbreviation for *er*, which a scribe misread, placing his expansion before instead of after the *t*. There are some astonishing variant readings among the manuscripts, all attempts to make sense of an absurd error: *sere trees, septres, Cereres, certis, centris, storyes, cercles*.³¹

The editorial process Robinson used to correct the Ellesmere text is known as emendation: substituting for an obvious error a better reading, or repairing a lacuna. It is easy to see how an editor experienced in dealing with manuscripts can know the reason for an error, and how he can identify the correct reading. Emendation is usually, but not always, done on the basis of manuscripts which are closely related. Also, editors sometimes make corrections on the basis of present-day knowledge of Middle English, for scribes frequently changed grammatical forms and added or dropped final *e*. Occasionally, and with great caution, an editor feels obliged to supply a correct reading himself, a procedure practiced more freely by medieval scribes. Examples of the medieval practice will be shown later in connection with Caxton's editing.³²

Returning to abbreviations, still others could be troublesome. An ambiguity in his exemplar, or a slip on his own part, could cause a scribe to confuse either a bar or a curve drawn through the stem of *p*: the difference between *parfit* and *profite* (Wife of Bath's Prologue, III, 92), in various forms, among the manuscripts.³³ Most notably of all, in the best-known line Chaucer ever wrote, generations of scholars read a bar through the Ellesmere scribe's double *l*, confirmed by other reliable manuscripts, as an abbreviated final *e* in *Aprill*, which is not etymologically justified.

Attempts to cope with words they did not understand sometimes led scribes to make blunders such as those already shown among the variant readings of the *sertres / sterres* error. Not less amusing are the evidences that some scribes encountered the Minotaur for the first time in the Knight's tale (I, 980): *Miniatan, Methan, Mytan, Manatour, Senatour*.³⁴ So, too, hamadryads, for whom Chaucer's spelling must have been close to the Ellesmere scribe's *amadrides* (Knight's tale, I, 2928): *amadriades, Amadryes*,

Amarides, Madrides, Madriades, Mydriades, armadriesse, amarindes.[35]

The scribe who copied a manuscript in which there is a particular error or ambiguity need not be the person responsible, for such situations were sometimes inherited from earlier scribes. Also, manuscripts can contain evidence of corrections by the author himself, and problems resulting from these. In Chaucer's case, no one should suppose on the basis of his career in the customs that he necessarily possessed meticulous habits of work when it came to composing poetry. He may have crowded corrections into his margins, or squeezed them into interlinear positions that were the despair of those who had to copy from his papers after his death. Indeed, he no doubt made his own share of errors. This, however, does not mean that he was other than a perfectionist about the poetry itself (or about his prose). That conclusion can certainly be drawn from the two prologues to the *Legend of Good Women*, each so worthy that distinguishing the original from the revision is an academic problem. *Troilus* and *Criseyde* was revised at least once, and there are scraps of evidence that several of the *Canterbury Tales* went through earlier drafts.

Manly and Rickert have listed a number of variant readings in the manuscripts of the *Canterbury Tales* believed to be substitutions, cancellations, and additions by Chaucer. An example of a word change occurs in the Knight's tale. Describing the pennant of Duke Theseus, Chaucer writes (I, 978-80),

> And by his baner born is his penoun
> Of gold ful riche, in which ther was ybete
> The Mynotaur, which that he slough in Crete.

The word *slough* is believed to be a substitution for an original reading, *wan*, found in the Hengwrt Manuscript.[36] It is known that there was an older version of the Knight's tale, for Chaucer refers to it in the Prologue of the *Legend of Good Women* (F, 420; G, 408), written before the period of the early *Canterbury Tales*.

~§ *Writing in Books*

In the Wife of Bath's Prologue, a passage now numbered editorially 44[a-f] was either added by Chaucer, as Manly and Rickert believe, or intended for cancellation, as Robinson thinks. Describing the selection of her five husbands, she says,

> Of whiche I have pyked out the beste,
> Bothe of here nether purs and of here cheste.
> Diverse scoles maken parfyt clerkes,
> And diverse practyk in many sondry werkes
> Maketh the werkman parfyt sekirly;
> Of fyve husbondes scoleiyng am I.

Whatever Chaucer meant to do with them, the lines are genuine. Robinson prints them as a footnote.[37]

Sometimes there is confusion regarding the correct location of lines, and in certain cases this may be because they were revisions by Chaucer, perhaps added in the margin of his own copy. In the Franklin's tale, the couplet V, 999-1000

> "Is ther noon oother grace in yow?" quod he.
> "No, by that Lord," quod she, "that maked me!"

appears in some manuscripts after line 1006.[38] Besides authors' corrections such as these, marginalia of various origins (glosses, or lines taken from other sources) could be copied inadvertently into a text by a scribe.

Although variant readings provide editors with many problems, they have a value of their own, for they can lead to the identification of variational, and ultimately genetic, groups of manuscripts. Also, manuscripts which have few of the common variants may have unique readings. By studying these variant readings, scholars can draw conclusions about the descent of a text, for usually all the manuscripts are derived by transcription from a single archetype, itself not necessarily the author's correct copy and hence not necessarily free from error. This archetype, and all its descendants, extant or not, in their interrelationships, form a "family," and hence can be studied in terms of genealogy.³⁹ By the process of recension—working backward through the lines of descent—editors can reconstruct the archetype of a given work. In the case of the *Canterbury Tales*, Manly and Rickert identified, on the basis of fifty-eight manuscripts which are relatively complete, four main genetic groups (a, b, c, d) and three manuscripts which are independently derived (Ellesmere, Hengwrt, and in part, Gg. 4. 27 of Cambridge University). By recension, they also established an archetype. Their results with regard to the archetype, however, are conditioned by the fact that Chaucer left no finished copy, so that the materials reached the earliest editors in various stages of composition and completeness. Thus, it becomes problematical whether one can indeed speak of a single archetype in this and similar cases.⁴⁰

While the genealogical method cannot reveal anything about the materials behind the archetype, it is used to establish the text of a work. In the case of the *Canterbury Tales*, this was unnecessary, for scholars had long known that the Ellesmere and Hengwrt manuscripts were the best. Copied from different exemplars within ten or twelve years of Chaucer's death, their general agreement, together with the care with which they were written, evidently by the same scribe, gives them the most prestigious position among the manuscripts, and implies that they stand closest to what Chaucer actually wrote. The Hengwrt Manuscript is thought to be the older of the two. Since the Ellesmere Manuscript is in better condition than the Hengwrt, which lacks some of the materials, it is customary to edit from the Ellesmere. Some of Chaucer's other works also present interesting problems to the editor, which will be discussed later in connection with Caxton's editing.⁴¹

Nothing is known about the circumstances under which Chaucer's writings were copied after his death in 1400. The scribe Adam's work must be somewhere in the history of the manuscripts of *Boece* and *Troilus*. Scholars have long been certain that the materials for the *Canterbury Tales* were found among Chaucer's papers, written either in fascicles or on single sheets of parchment or paper, and that the archetype, if in fact there was only

✢§ *Writing in Books*

one, was prepared from these.[42] This, of course, does not rule out other possibilities, such as a joint editorial undertaking by Chaucer's friends, some of whom were poets, made from materials in their own possession. But there is no manuscript certain to be the archetype or a copy of it. Nor does any manuscript have more authority than its own prestige for the order in which the materials are presented. It is well known that a more logical order can be achieved by the shift recommended by Henry Bradshaw, in which Fragment VII would be made to follow Fragment II, the Man of Law's tale and endlink.[43]

Although traditionally the role of the scribes was faithful reproduction of an exemplar, it was common for them (or for their supervisors) to make changes in spelling and grammar, to correct obvious errors, and to edit unintelligible situations. In Chaucer's case, editing was sometimes done by persons whose lack of ability would be laughable were it not for the damage done to the poet's text. It is, of course, easy to criticize another age for lack of professionalism. Fifteenth-century scribes labored under rapid changes in the language that must have made it very difficult to understand Chaucer's pronunciation and hence his versification. Admiring imitation, then a tribute to a master, also made it difficult to distinguish authentic from imitative, and even forged, materials. The *Canterbury Tales*, in particular, were subjected to wholesale editing. Lines, links, and at least one entire tale *(Gamelyn)* were inadvertently or deliberately added, or even forged, in some manuscripts, no doubt to satisfy patrons.[44] By the time the printer Caxton appeared upon the scene in the late fifteenth century, the manuscripts of the *Canterbury Tales* were infested with problems of authorial, scribal, and editorial origin, some of which may never be solved.

Yet this should not detract from the overall merit of the medieval scribes' labors. Considering the state of the materials they had to work with in many cases, and the conditions under which they performed their task, their contribution to literature by the preservation of texts is remarkable. Their work is by and large accurate, attractive, and efficient and in most cases, the writing can be read after only moderate amounts of training. When Chaucer complained of his scribe's mistakes, it was in verses difficult to take other than in the spirit of good humor.

NOTES TO CHAPTER 3

[1] The standard work on paleography is Edward Maunde Thompson, *An Introduction to Greek and Latin Palaeography* (Oxford, 1912). Excellent introductory essays are Elias Avery Lowe, "Handwriting," in *The Legacy of the Middle Ages*, ed. Charles George Crump and Ernest Fraser Jacob (Oxford, 1943), pp. 197-226; and Vivian Hunter Galbraith, "Handwriting," in Austin Lane Poole, ed., *Medieval England*, new ed., rev. (Oxford, 1958), II, 541-58.

[2] *The Rule of Saint Benedict*, trans. Francis Aidan [Cardinal] Gasquet (London, 1909), pp. 84-87.

[3] In addition to the work of Maunde Thompson, an excellent basic study of the book arts in classical times is Frederic George Kenyon, *Books and Readers in Ancient Greece and Rome* (Oxford, 1932).

[4] For capitals, uncials, and half-uncials, see Lowe, "Handwriting," Plate 25.

[5] Cursive writing is discussed by Thompson, *Greek and Latin Palaeography*, pp. 148-97 (Greek); 310-39 (Latin); 491-570 (official and legal cursive scripts).

[6] Hilary Jenkinson, *The Later Court Hands in England* (Cambridge, 1927); Malcolm Beckwith Parkes, *English Cursive Book Hands 1250-1500* (Oxford, 1969).

[7] *'Black Letter' Text* (Cambridge, 1942), p. 8.

[8] Lowe, "Handwriting," Plate 26 (a). See also *Evangeliorum Quattuor Codex Cenannensis* (Berne, Switzerland, 1950: the Book of Kells, facsimile edition).

[9] Lowe, Plate 26 (b). See also *Evangeliorum Quattuor Codex Lindisfarnensis* (Olten, Switzerland, 1956: the Lindisfarne Gospels, facsimile edition).

[10] Lowe, Plates 27, 28.

[11] For linguistic discussion of these symbols, see Fernand Mossé, *A Handbook of Middle English*, trans. James A. Walker (Baltimore, 1952), pp. 8-12. For historical discussion of runes, see Ralph W. V. Elliott, *Runes: An Introduction* (Manchester, 1959).

Writing in Books

[12] For Insular (vernacular), see Galbraith, "Handwriting," Plate 115.

[13] Lowe, Plate 36.

[14] Margaret Rickert, *Painting in Britain: The Middle Ages* (London, 1954), Plates 83-85.

[15] See also Lowe, Plates 37, 38.

[16] Galbraith, p. 548. For full discussion, see Thompson, pp. 71-74 (tachygraphy); 75-90 (abbreviations and contractions).

[17] The authoritative work on manuscript abbreviations is Adriano Cappelli, *Dizionario di abbreviature latine ed italiane* (Milan, 1929). Although this work is in Italian, the examples are self-explanatory and a reading knowledge of Italian is not essential.

[18] *English Cursive Book Hands*, p. xiii. See below, 93.

[19] Ibid., xxvi; xiv. The descriptions which ensue follow Parkes.

[20] Ibid, Plates 7, 8.

[21] Ibid., Plates 11-13.

[22] Transcriptions are provided for plates containing text.

[23] M-R, IV, 76, 490.

[24] Ibid., 293, 520.

[25] M-R, III, 280, 451.

[26] Ibid., 119, 436; V, 289.

[27] M-R, IV, 288, 519; VIII, 12.

[28] Martin Michael Crow, "John of Angoulême and His Chaucer Manuscript," *Speculum*, 17 (1942), 86-99. See also M-R, I, 399-405.

[29] M-R, III, 111, 434-35; V, 264.

[30] See below, p. 84.

[31] M-R, III, 86, 432; V, 196.

[32] See below, pp. 130-31.

[33] M-R, III, 239, 455; VI, 13; see above, p. 65.

[34] M-R, III, 44-45; V, 92.

[35] M-R, III, 118, 436; V, 287.

[36] M-R, II, 38-39; III, 45; V, 92.

[37] M-R, II, 38-39; III, 236, 454-55; VI, 7-8. See also Robinson, p. 891.

[38] M-R, II, 38-39; IV, 43; VI, 606.

[39] Walter Wilson Greg, *The Calculus of Variants* (Oxford, 1927), p. 1. Greg's essay is of maximum difficulty, but the first five pages are especially useful for their clarification of terminology. For bibliography, and for criticism of the genealogical method, see M-R, II, 12-20.

[40] M-R, II, 12-45; for their archetype, with critical notes, see III, IV.

[41] See below, pp. 125-33.

[42] The authoritative discussion of the subject is that of John Strong Perry Tatlock, "The *Canterbury Tales* in 1400," *PMLA*, 50 (1935), 100-39.

[43] The authoritative study of the order of the *Canterbury Tales* is that of Robert Armstrong Pratt, "The Order of the *Canterbury Tales*," *PMLA*, 66 (1951), 1141-67.

[44] For discussion, see William Symington McCormick, and Janet E. Heseltine, "A Study of the Links and Some Outstanding Divergencies of Arrangement in the Manuscripts of the *Canterbury Tales*," *The Manuscripts of the "Canterbury Tales"* (Oxford, 1933), pp. xv-xxxii.

4
Book Trade and Libraries

IN THE PROLOGUE to the *Legend of Good Women,* Chaucer's persona acknowledges, through the god of love, that he owns sixty books. The god says (G, 273-77),

> Yis, God wot, sixty bokes olde and newe
> Hast thow thyself, alle ful of storyes grete,
> That bothe Romayns and ek Grekes trete
> Of sundry wemen, which lyf that they ladde,
> And evere an hundred goode ageyn oon badde.

Sixty books need not mean sixty volumes, since it was customary to bind together books not necessarily related, and in his lifetime Chaucer probably owned more than the number specified. But sixty books, in whatever form, was a goodly collection for a private citizen who was not rich, and one can only wish that he had provided a list.

Following the custom of the time, Chaucer doubtless had books copied for his library. He is his own witness that he employed a scribe. While some books could have been gifts, it goes without saying that he also bought books, both in England and in the course of his travels abroad. But there is no reason to suppose that he owned all that he knew or knew about. Presumably, he borrowed from acquaintances, and presumably he was familiar with some important libraries. Both the book trade and libraries of the time are part of Chaucer's background; they are at least the frame of the all-but-unknown story of the descent of his works into and through the fifteenth century.

It would be a mistake to imply that there was, even in the fifteenth century, an organized book trade comparable to anything familiar to us now.[1] The book trade of the time is best understood in terms of its development. As discussed earlier, accident had placed the entire enterprise of publishing in the hands of the monasteries after the fall of Rome.[2] The monastic scriptorium was nothing at all new, but was a perpetuation of the system of copying as it had been under the Greeks and Romans, who had employed an elite type of slave for the work of reproducing manuscripts. Both worlds had a supply of free labor for the purpose, which, in the case of monasteries, made possible the accumulation of libraries when writing materials, as well as books, were both expensive and hard to obtain. In maintaining communications among themselves, the monasteries provided avenues for the exchange of books, which were sometimes copied to order for outside clients. While this cannot be described as a commercial enterprise in the modern business sense, it is book trade nevertheless, and the monasteries must be regarded both as the first medieval publishers and as the main arteries for the distribution of books in early times.

But secular persons also had a part in this rudimentary book trade. Pedlars carried books among their wares, and there was a market for books at fairs, both on the Continent and in England.[3] By the thirteenth century, the fair at Sturbridge (Stourbridge), near Cambridge, was the most important one in England, comparable to those of Leipzig, Novgorod, and Troyes, and it was the one in particular where books were bought and sold.[4] This, however, was a trade in used books. While the marketing of books produced for open sale has no specific recorded history, it did not become anything like standard procedure before the advent of printing.

Monastic scriptoria continued to produce books throughout the Middle Ages and later, but not as a monopoly. By the thirteenth century the universities had established control over the books used on their own premises through a closely regulated publishing enterprise. An agent known as a stationer was licensed

Book Trade and Libraries

by the faculty to produce master copies of authorized textbooks. These could not be sold so long as the books were in use, but they could be rented to members of the academic community, who could take them in fascicles (*peciae*) and make their own copies.[5]

The *pecia* system has a particular application here, not only as part of the standard procedure for marketing books in the later Middle Ages, but also as important evidence regarding the famous collection of Aristotles belonging to Chaucer's Clerk of Oxford. The need for some system of enabling students, always notoriously impecunious, to obtain textbooks, is obvious. Even though university enrollments were small compared with those of today, the nature of manuscript books was such that no library could have supplied all comers with facilities for study. Lending, now taken for granted, was very restricted in medieval libraries, and books, when loaned at all, customarily circulated only upon deposit of a pledge, greater in value than the books concerned. University libraries were not exceptions, though there were usually statutes insuring free lending to certain poor students and to regents.

The *pecia* was not set up to look like a separate entity. Although the beginning of each *pecia* is carefully indicated by a mark, an unpracticed eye would not recognize a manuscript intended as an exemplar. Among specific characteristics, the manuscripts written in *peciae* are always in Latin, always on academic subjects, and of the thirteenth century or later. The parchment used for these master copies was not of high quality. The greatest investment was in the writing, which was Gothic, and in the correcting, the exemplars being notable for their accuracy—necessarily so, since heavy penalties awaited the stationer who rented inaccurate or incomplete materials. H. E. Bell gives the cost ratio between the parchment and the copying at 1:5.[6] He has calculated a fairly consistent rate of 6,200 words per shilling for copying academic books.[7]

With regard to the rentals charged for the master copies, which were set, not by the stationer but by the university, there are few lists giving the number of *peciae* and the fee, but one from Paris

(1275), printed by Destrez, includes, among other works, the commentaries of Thomas Aquinas upon the four books of Peter Lombard's *Sentences* as follows: "on the first book, 36 *peciae*, 2 *sous*; on the second, 47 *peciae*, 2 *sous*; on the third, 1 *pecia*, 2 *sous*; on the fourth, 81 *peciae*, 4 *sous*."[8] In these calculations, the relative cash values are: *livre* (pound)=20 *sous*; *sou*=12 *deniers*, the last being the smallest denomination used in France. These are, of course, rental fees, not sales prices. The *peciae* seem to have been borrowed and paid for individually. Destrez prints records showing students managing (and mismanaging) their debts for these with stationers.[9] Under the *pecia* system, a student, such as Chaucer's Clerk of Oxford, could have provided himself with a respectable collection of textbooks at no extravagant cost, especially since the stationer was also obliged to sell him parchment at a discount—this despite the fact that one scholar has valued the Clerk's collection of Aristotles at several burghers' houses, another at an orchestra of "fithele or gay sautrie."[10]

The university stationers, also called *librarii*, must have been able to earn a good living. Although they had to submit to university regulation, they were subsidized, given benefit of clergy (for themselves, not for their families), and provided with a captive clientele, for students could not work without textbooks. The first Oxford stationer whose name is a matter of record is one Robert, located in Cat Street in 1308. By 1374, however, the number of bookmen had increased to include some who were not, properly speaking, university stationers, and the university found it necessary to decree that none except those sworn to the institution could sell any book exceeding half a mark in value.[11] Whatever else this may mean, its immediate significance is the indication that persons whose estate as clergy was merely a legal convenience not only engaged in the book business but did so in numbers, the implication being that there was profit in books.

The book trade in Chaucer's England was not, however, university oriented or controlled. Aristocrats and wealthy burgesses were acquiring vernacular books in the fourteenth and fifteenth centuries, and from sources that were secular. The nobility had long been obtaining richly illuminated psalters and books of hours. Now, the rise of the English middle classes to affluence produced an urban market for books, especially for English translations and for originally vernacular literature. Chaucer himself made English translations of two works which were in his day among the most important and popular: the *Roman de la Rose* and the *De Consolatione Philosophiae*. Nor was this market confined to the middle classes. It is well known that the nobility read and valued English Literature. As for the common man, J. W. Adamson long ago demonstrated that literacy was much more prevalent than was once supposed.[12] But ownership of books does not necessarily follow from literacy, and Margaret Deanesly concludes from a study of 7,600 wills that the English were still a people largely bookless, more so in the fourteenth century than in the fifteenth.[13]

But the market for books was indeed growing. Publishing was becoming an increasingly secular enterprise, and scriptoria, under pressure to supply an expanding market for books, speeded up production by whatever means they could find. In England, a milestone in this history is the much-discussed Auchinleck Manuscript (Advocates MS. 19. 2. 1, National Library, Edinburgh). Cheaply produced by a team of five scribes in a secular scriptorium of London somewhat before 1340, this collection of metrical romances is important as a sourcebook for allusions in Chaucer's "Sir Thopas," and some have believed that Chaucer knew the book.[14] Regardless of that, the Auchinleck Manuscript shows that secular stationers were at work in London in the second quarter of the fourteenth century, and that there was then a market for bourgeois literature, such as Chaucer satirizes in "Sir Thopas."

A century later, secular scriptoria were doing a flourishing business. On the Continent, this had much to do with the impact of Italian humanism, for scholars had begun to search for manuscripts of lost or rare classical works, and to collect the works of classical authors, which meant that copies had to be made. The most famous name among Continental stationers is that of Vespasiano da Bisticci. In the mid-fifteenth century, he had a large staff of scribes, illuminators, and binders, capable of turning out two hundred manuscripts for one patron in less than two years.

This Vespasiano was no ordinary stationer. He was a connoisseur of books, who advised great men on their libraries. He was also a biographer; his *Vite di uomini illustri* contained sketches of important people he knew. He was instrumental in finding rare books for his clients, especially Greek and Latin classics, and he specialized in having Latin translations prepared from the Greek. Thus he became an important figure in Italian humanism, his one shortcoming being a total inability to see the possibilities printing offered to the cause of learning—perhaps a justifiable response to the threat to his own business in manuscripts. Nevertheless, it was the humanist script used by his scribes which eventually became the model of the so-called roman style of type.[15]

In England, the name of the London stationer John Shirley is best known.[16] He is of particular interest to the present study because he personally copied at least two miscellanies containing, among other pieces, works by Chaucer: Additional MS. 16165, British Museum (*Boece*, "Anelida and Arcite") and MS. R. 3. 20, Trinity College, Cambridge ("Anelida and Arcite"). There are six extant Shirley manuscripts, all written on paper, his handwriting readily recognized by odd flourishes on letters having stems. Some books of his atelier have a stanza known as his "book-plate," which has been attributed to Lydgate:

> Yee that desyre in herte and have plesaunce
> Olde stories in bokis for to rede
> Gode matieres putt hem in remembraunce
> And of the other take yee none hede
> Bysechyng yowe of youre godely hede
> Whanne yee this boke have over-redde and seyne
> To *Johan Shirley* restore yee hit ageyne.[17]

The implication is that Shirley was a lender of books. At the time of his death in 1456, he was tenant of a large house and four shops rented from St. Bartholomew's Hospital, believed to have been the location of his atelier. So little is known about him that there

◆§ *Book Trade and Libraries*

is no way of comparing him with other important stationers of the time. Indeed, there may be no comparison with people like Vespasiano, for no books of truly excellent quality survive from Shirley's scriptorium. That he was acquainted with both Lydgate and Thomas Chaucer, believed to have been the poet's son, makes him a link in the chain which Brusendorff has called "the Chaucer tradition."[18] While the names of other scribes are associated with Chaucer manuscripts, Shirley is the only one about whom even this much biographical information can be discovered.

Far less is known about the businesses of urban stationers in England this early than is known about those of stationers affiliated with universities. In London an organization ancestral to the Company of Stationers existed in 1403, traced by some authorities to the even earlier date of 1357.[19] Also, there were independent persons who did work connected with book production, especially copying, whose identity is usually revealed only by autographs in manuscripts and by mention in account books. The nobility and wealthy bourgeoisie employed professional scribes to write their documents and accounts, as did men of letters such as Chaucer, and monasteries were sometimes obliged to hire professionals for all kinds of copying, including the copying of books.

The kind of wage paid for such services was, in general, on a level with wages paid for agricultural work. Doing far better than average was the scribe employed by Westminster Abbey for copying the missal now known by the name of Abbot Nicholas Lytlington. He received £4 for two years' work. Bell estimates that the missal contains 250,000 words, and that it was therefore copied at 3,100 words per shilling.[20] Since liturgical books required meticulous writing, and since this missal is large, the scribe may or may not have averaged a shilling's work a day. If he did, he was highly paid for the time, doing better than carpenters, masons, and the best-paid agricultural workers. As already noted, copyists of academic books averaged a shilling for 6,200 words, which, bearing in mind the premium for accuracy in exemplars, must have been at least two days' work. This amounts to 6*d*. for one day.[21] In general, such work could be hired for a set period with a stipend, perhaps with board and lodging, or it could be paid for by the piece. In 1372, a scribe at Ely received £2. 3s. 4d. for the year, and at St. George's, Windsor, in the same year, a scribe received 13s. 4d. for eighteen weeks.[22] It would be interesting to know what Chaucer paid the scribe Adam.

The varied conditions under which books could be acquired in the fourteenth and fifteenth centuries render extremely difficult any attempt to generalize about the cash value of books. The prices paid for books were as much a matter of agreement between the parties involved in the transaction as a matter of custom. Records are found almost anywhere, useful sources being notes on flyleaves (where successive owners frequently entered their prices), catalogs of libraries, wills, inventories, and account books such as those of churchwardens and stationers. But such records do not always reflect sales prices or actual cash transactions. Records of university stationers which pertain to exemplars reflect rentals, not sales, while libraries, which had to protect their holdings by requiring pledges for their loans, overvalued their books to take care of the common practice of requiring pledges greater in value than the book loaned. While there is entertainment value and antiquarian interest in the documents that actually contain the records, reprinting these in great numbers would be of little profit here. Price ranges are more important for present purposes, and these are best studied in terms of classification of books, since there is very little in common between, for example, a missal and a copy of the *Roman de la Rose*. For purposes of the present study, books will be classified as Bell classifies them: liturgical, academic, and popular.

Liturgical books are texts of the Church's official public services. Thus, a missal is a liturgical book. The chief customers for most liturgical books—missals, antiphoners, pontificals, graduals, and the like—were institutions: parish churches, cathedrals, and monasteries. Though the nobility and the very wealthy bourgeoisie might find use for some of these works if they had a private chapel, the principal liturgical and devotional books possessed by individuals were psalters, breviaries, and books of hours.

⇒§ Book Trade and Libraries

There were numerous attempts in the Middle Ages to produce a standard, uniform breviary, or text of the Divine Office, but this was a product of later times.[23]

The cash value of liturgical books was an entirely relative matter. An institution such as Westminster Abbey, seeking a monumental work for its sanctuary, could and did have one made to order rather than have one purchased on the open market. Its Lytlington Missal, copied in 1383-84, cost, as already noted, £4 for the services of the scribe, £22. 0s. 3d. for the illumination, and a total of £2. 7s. 4d. for various jobs connected with binding.[24] There can be no generalizations, however, about the price of such missals as were bought and sold. This depended upon many factors, such as the lavishness or plainness of the book, its condition, and the persons involved in the transaction. A fifteenth-century list records prices of thirteen missals from £2 to £4, and the same number from above £4 to £10.[25] These prices are best understood in terms of other costs involved in publishing, as for instance the fact that the scribe of the Lytlington missal received £4 for his services. From £2 to £4 was an expensive purchase, but certainly within the means of an institution. A really poor parish priest could doubtless have found himself a worn but respectable missal which he could afford.

The missal was the most important of the Church's liturgical books: without it, all would have come to a stop, since it contained the text of the Mass, the movable parts of which are beyond anyone's power of memory. The costs of other sanctuary books, depending upon their size and luxury, tended to run higher than those of missals. The reason is the extra cost of musical notation as well as the positive need for large size so that they could be held up or placed on a lectern for use by several persons at a time. This is particularly true of antiphoners, used by choirs. Again from a fifteenth-century list, Bell notes that seventeen of thirty-nine antiphoners were priced from £5 to £10, two being more expensive. Of the lower priced ones, he omits those which were either very old or printed. Making similar exceptions, he eliminates eight of thirty-five graduals, noting that twenty-two of the remainder cost

97

between £2 and £4.²⁶ Other very specialized sanctuary books need not be considered here.

Bibles could also be liturgical books, and they were often copied in parts so that they could be written in large letters and conveniently used. But Bibles had another use, as academic books. Thus, there are enormous differences in the manner in which Bibles were presented. Bell has assembled prices of thirty-nine, distributed over the period 1300-1530. Eliminating three as special cases, he shows the prices of thirty-six: twenty-three range from £2 to £4; eight cost over £4, and five cost less than £2. The highest price Bell has found was paid by the Abbot of Croxden in 1276: 50 marks.²⁷ Some Bibles, specifically those for academic purposes, were glossed, an operation involving additional costs.

While the missal is the one liturgical book commonly known now to the public at large, citizens of the Middle Ages would have been more familiar with books of hours. Like breviaries, they exhibit wide variation in luxury or its opposite, and it is useless to attempt any price range as there is no norm as to what might be paid. The same is true of breviaries. Bell finds at Winchester breviaries priced under £1, and one at the same place worth £20.²⁸ Books of hours were short, and could be had for a few shillings, though there was no limit to the splendor that could be lavished on these works by the artists who worked for the nobility, such as Jean Pucelle and his atelier.

Academic books served purposes quite apart from those which called forth the decorative arts that frequently enhanced liturgical books, and their usefulness was enhanced by smaller size. Many of the available statistics are obscured by the rental prices of the *pecia* system, and by the medieval custom of dividing books into parts, which might be bound with other materials. Bell gives some interesting statistics nevertheless. Of nine priced copies of St. Augustine's *De Civitate Dei*, six cost between £1 and £2; of ten priced copies of Gregory the Great's *Pastoralia*, seven cost 2s. to 4s.; of the *Historia Scholastica*, he finds eighteen priced from £1 to £1. 10s, one luxury copy recorded at a higher figure.²⁹ The sum of £1 was a great deal of money in those days when several pennies,

ಳ್ಳಿ Book Trade and Libraries

or even one, represented a day's wage. What the records do not show is the probable underground market of dilapidated copies that went for a few pennies and never saw a stationer's shelves.

It is interesting that there exists a list of popular books, mostly romances, that belonged to Richard II in 1384-85, many of them priced. While romances, like any other books, could be made to order at whatever expense the patron had in mind, the list which follows shows books which must be reckoned inexpensive in comparison with the kinds that have been discussed. Nothing is said about the telling matters of size, length, or bindings, but some of these works are well known, and a great deal can be learned from the fact that a copy of the *Roman de la Rose* good enough for a king's library could be had, at least by him, for 20s. The rest of the priced list follows, here given as annotated by its editor, Edith Rickert, because some of the works named are of uncertain identity:

> Item une [*elsewhere un*] Romance de Roy Arthure pris. xl. s. (Le Livre d'Artus?)
>
> Item un Romance de Emery de Nerbon pris. xxvij. s. viij. d. (Aimeri de Narbonne)
>
> Item un Romance de Trebor pris. xx. s. (the A. N. Enseignements Trebor, by Robert de Ho)
>
> Item un Romance de Lorhens Garryn pris. xxvj. s. viij. d. (Garin le Lorrain)
>
> Item un Romance de Darry & ffloridas pris. xx. s. (? Roman de Daurel)
>
> Item un livre des laies mons' Lowys Counte de Cleremond pris. iij. s. iiij. d.
>
> Item un Romance de Generides pris. vj. s. viij. d. (known by two English translations)
>
> Item un Romance de fferers & Garders pris. ij. s.
>
> Item un livre appelle Galaath pris. x. s. (some form of the Queste del Saint Graal)
>
> Item un autre livre comensant 'Ap's ce q'Henriz' pris. vj. s. viij. d.
>
> Item un Romance q'comence 'Seignours voillez oier un bon Chauncon' pris. vj. s. viij. d. (a common beginning for late *chansons de geste*)

On the back is a short list of the same date, including a copy of the *Romance of the Rose* as noted above and also "un Romance de Percevall & Gawyn pris. vj. s. viij. d."[30] Needless to say, books presented much more expensively also reposed in the royal collections and in those of other wealthy persons. Certainly, a luxuriously illustrated Chaucer, such as the Ellesmere Manuscript, must have cost its original owner a great deal of money.

Aside from what they bought locally, the English also obtained books by buying abroad. Richard de Bury, the noted bibliophile of Chaucer's century, bought books in Paris, then the center of the book trade, and he sent agents, especially members of the mendicant orders, to buy for him all over Europe. The fact that he was himself sent to Paris on diplomatic business was undoubtedly a political reward, which is not to say that he was without qualifications for the post.[31] The precedent is not to be overlooked in Chaucer's case, for in the same capacity he visited Italy, and he is known to have gone to Milan, Venice, and Florence, the most important centers of the book trade in the second half of his century.

In the fifteenth century, the mercers, about whom more will be said later in connection with Caxton, traded in books as well as in textiles, importing them from Bruges as luxury items. Caxton himself imported books after he opened his printing establishment in Westminster.[32] But the chief importers of books in his time were Peter Actors (later the king's stationer), Henry Franckenbergk, Barnard von Stondo, and Andrew Rue.[33] The king must have decided to encourage the businesses of bookmen, including foreigners, for the terms of an act of 1484 permit any foreign bookseller or printer to import books, and any foreign scribe, illuminator, or bookbinder to live and work in England.[34] As for prices, although records are scarce before the sixteenth century, printed books could cost almost anything. They were not necessarily cheaper than manuscripts, though the relative cheapness of paper compared with the cost of parchment meant that this was often the case.[35] While records of Caxton's prices are scarce, fifteen copies of his *Golden Legend* (presumably the second edition) were sold

Book Trade and Libraries

in 1496, about five years after his death, at prices ranging between 6s. 4d. and 6s. 8d., these no doubt based on current prices of books of the same general kind.[36]

Consideration of the book trade would not be complete without attention to its customers, and therefore to libraries. To explore this vast and important topic, it is necessary to begin with the monastic library, which was the heir of classical tradition on the one hand, and on the other hand the precedent for dealing with books until much later times.[37] Before the fourteenth and fifteenth centuries, monastic libraries were little more than chests or closets (presses), called *armaria*, located along the cloister wall, where glazed bays provided light and were accordingly fitted with carrels for reading. In these locked *armaria*, books were stored flat. The best information about such library fittings comes from pictorial representations, for most early library furnishings were eventually replaced and destroyed.

The precentor, whose charge over liturgical volumes extended to other books, was also, at least in earlier times, *armarius* or librarian. He was under strict rules regarding the management of the books in his charge. These rules, of course, varied greatly from institution to institution. Earliest, they concerned chiefly the observance of St. Benedict's mandate that every monk receive a book from the library to read through during Lent, with the consequent keeping of records.[38] There were also regulations for the precentor's duties in keeping the *armaria* and their contents clean and in good repair, and in teaching the same to the younger monks. Books could not be borrowed without careful record. As for lending to outsiders, the customs of the Benedictines of Abingdon are typical: the precentor is forbidden to sell, give away, or pledge any book. He is likewise forbidden to lend, except to neighboring churches "vel excellentibus personis," which excellence no doubt refers to wealth, since he is required to obtain a pledge of equal or greater value than the book itself.[39]

Manuscripts not infrequently ended with a nudge to the reader's conscience in the form of a curse, in the event that redemption of his pledge was not enough to make him return it. These imprecations are doubtless more amusing now than in the age when they were written, as the following examples demonstrate:

> This book belongs to S. Maximin at his monastery of Micy, which abbat Peter caused to be written, and with his own labour corrected and punctuated, and on Holy Thursday dedicated to God and S. Maximin on the altar of S. Stephen, with this imprecation that he who should take it away from thence by what device soever, with the intention of not restoring it, should incur damnation with the traitor Judas, with Annas, Caiaphas, and Pilate. Amen.[40]

The monastery of St. Albans had a standard formula to protect its books:

> This book belongs to St. Alban. May whosoever steals it from him or destroys its title be anathema. Amen.[41]

The holdings of a monastic library would include, besides the liturgical books that properly belonged to the sacristy, suitable fare for the monks' spiritual reading, and books for the school, if there was one. Beyond that, such a library could contain practically anything, depending upon the interests of past abbots and upon bequests, since people sometimes willed their personal libraries to ecclesiastical institutions. The exact number of volumes such an establishment had at a particular date can often be ascertained, but the information is misleading because of the custom of binding together diverse books into a single volume. Actually, there was no real reason for a community of monks to have an extensive library, and many monasteries must have had very few books. On the other hand, collections large for their times existed at certain houses. In 831, the Benedictines of St. Riquier had 250 volumes. A century later, Bobbio had about 700 manuscripts. In the twelfth century, Durham had 366 volumes.[42] In later times such libraries were much larger. The number of volumes, of course, does not reveal the count of separate manuscripts, which is likely to have been about three times larger.

Needless to say, collections of books had to be cataloged. At

Book Trade and Libraries

St. Martin's Priory, Dover, in 1389, the books were divided among nine presses (*armaria*), designated by the first nine letters of the alphabet, each press being divided into seven shelves, designated by Roman numerals. At Christ Church, Canterbury, one of the largest libraries in the country, the books were first divided into ten "demonstrations," or large general divisions.[43] Christ Church had about 1850 manuscripts in 1331.[44] Other major ecclesiastical libraries were those of St. Albans, Bury St. Edmunds, and Durham. A complete list of important ecclesiastical libraries Chaucer could have known would be very long indeed.

The universities were heirs to the monastic system of keeping libraries. Universities had problems very different from those of monastic libraries, whose clients were chiefly persons obliged to remain within the same premises. Students were under no such obligation. Their need to obtain books was active, rather than contemplative, and at times desperate. Having actual, and not merely ideal, poverty to goad them, they represented the worst of all possible borrowers of books, so that universities, with their limited library facilities, could not have functioned without the *pecia* system to take the strain off their holdings.

These libraries did lend books to certain students, and to regents, upon pledge. More important, however, was the custom of placing books upon lecterns and securing them with chains, so that they could be used freely without risk of theft. Chained libraries, which were not peculiar to universities, certainly existed in the fourteenth century, and were usual in the fifteenth. The chains were attached to an iron bar, slotted through, and locked into, finials at the top of the lectern. Ideally the chain ended in a swivel, to prevent entanglement. This was attached to a ring, which was strung upon the bar, and the book itself carried a loop for the chain, attached to its cover by means of a rivet.[45]

A chained library was cataloged somewhat differently from a library in which the books were kept in presses. At Queen's College, Cambridge, in 1472, there were 192 volumes, divided among ten desks and four half desks (each called *gradus* 'step,' a term previously used for shelf). J. W. Clark estimates the count as eight volumes on each half desk and fifteen on each complete desk.[46] In earliest times the books were kept flat, but later the lectern system evolved into tall bookcases, and the books were stood upright with their spines facing into the cases.

The collections of university libraries, and their size, exhibited great variation. At King's Hall, Cambridge, in 1394, there were 87 volumes. In the following century, St. Catherine's Hall had 104, King's College, 175, and Peterhouse, 380.[47]

Library facilities built to accommodate books and readers belong chiefly to the fifteenth century. At Christ Church, Canterbury, a library about 60 feet long by 22 feet wide was built between 1414 and 1443 over the Prior's chapel. At Durham, *ca.* 1446, a room over the old sacristy was either built or rebuilt as a library, the room being 44 feet 10 inches long by 18 feet wide, with a window at each end. At St. Albans the library was begun in 1452 and finished the next year, at a cost of £150. The original library of St. Paul's Cathedral, London, was of the time of Henry VI. At Merton College, Oxford, founded in 1264, the library was not begun until 1377; at University College, founded 1280, in 1440. The first such library included in an original plan was that of New College, Oxford, 1380.[48] It can be concluded from this summary that library structures built to accommodate both books and those who wished to read them were not known in Chaucer's youth, and that even in his later life, they were not normally part of the milieu of books.

As for private libraries, there must have been many individuals in Chaucer's century who collected books. While Richard de Bury was certainly not the first Englishman to do so, he was the first to collect on a large scale. His library is reputed to have contained about 1500 items. Chaucer must have known of the bibliophile bishop of Durham, and he had probably seen his books, which had been willed to Durham College, Oxford, later abolished by Henry VIII. Robert A. Pratt has also made a good case for the likelihood that the poet knew one of the best libraries in Europe: that of the Visconti, at Milan.[49] In 1378, it will be remembered, Chaucer was sent to Milan on a diplomatic mission involv-

Book Trade and Libraries

ing Bernabò Visconti. He must have admired Bernabò, for in the Monk's tale (VII, 2400), he calls him "God of delit, and scourge of Lumbardye." Bernabò's brother, Galeazzo II, afterwards moved to Pavia, where he had a library reckoned in 1426 at 988 volumes, and Bernabò's is thought to have been comparable, although it was destroyed in 1385 when his castle was sacked. Since Petrarch lived eight years in Milan, Pratt regards it as inevitable that the Visconti owned literary books, and he suggests that it was in their library that Chaucer first read Boccaccio. But Chaucer need not have actually borrowed such books from the Visconti in order to read Italian poets, for Milan was then an important center of the book trade, and the poet would have been able to buy or order copies of works by Boccaccio. For that matter, Bernabò may have given such books to an English emissary who was also a poet.

But attempting to connect Chaucer with any particular English library would be mere speculation, for the life records are silent upon the subject of whatever formal education Chaucer may have had, as they are upon the subject of his intellectual pursuits. Scholars have clutched at straws attempting to connect him with the universities, the Inner Temple (where law was studied), and the school of St. Paul's Cathedral.[50] This last case is particularly interesting, not because it is true or false, but because the documents upon which Edith Rickert based her belief that Chaucer went to school there have another importance in that they show what kind of books an intellectual might own. Among the Cathedral archives are two handsome bequests from former schoolmasters. William de Tolleshurst (d. 1328) left twenty or thirty books, mostly on grammar, logic, natural history, medicine, and law. William de Ravenstone (d. 1358) bequeathed eighty-four books in forty-three or forty-four volumes. Of these, the inventory merely enumerates eighteen without description, perhaps because they were popular literature. The rest are works by such authors as Avianus, Theodulus, Maximian, Claudian, Lucan, Juvenal, Persius, Statius, Horace, Ovid, Cato, Aristotle, Donatus, and Priscian.[51]

While it is obvious that a change of emphasis separates the two collections, and that the second is what would now be called humanistic, the fact that England was still medieval and conservative long after Chaucer's death in 1400 is supported by the reactions of the first Italian humanist to go there in the fifteenth century. Poggio Bracciolini went to England in 1418, sponsored by Cardinal Beaufort, for the purpose of searching for rare classical books reputedly hidden away in English libraries. He found almost nothing, and left disappointed both with Englishmen and their libraries. It was not the peregrinations of Italian scholars, but the persistence of dazzled English bibliophiles which, in the first half of the fifteenth century, moved England toward Italian humanism.[52] This matter is relevant to the present study because it must be assumed, although it cannot be proved, that the libraries of these English collectors contained works by so celebrated a poet as Chaucer. By the end of the century Caxton was drawing support for his printing business, which specialized in books either written in or translated into English, from precisely such clients.

First among English bibliophiles of the fifteenth century, and most famous of all, was Humphrey, duke of Gloucester, the "Good Duke."[53] So renowned has Duke Humphrey become for the books he gave to Oxford that his political career is all but forgotten, even though he was regent of England (1417) and a major strategist during the wars with France. Popular with the middle classes, especially with the citizens of London, he fell under suspicion during the reign of Henry VI for precisely this reason, and his fall from power was precipitated by the implication of his wife, Eleanor Cobham, in a witchcraft trial. He died, or more probably was murdered, while attending the King at Bury St. Edmunds (1447).

Like Richard de Bury, Humphrey left no stone unturned to obtain money to spend on books. He had been introduced to humanism by his friend, Zenone da Castiglione, bishop of Bayeux, but enthusiasm for books had certainly existed in his family earlier. His father, Henry IV, and his brothers, Henry V and John, duke of Bedford, were all bibliophiles and Henry IV had

Book Trade and Libraries

granted Chaucer an annuity in 1399. The beautiful Campsall Manuscript of *Troilus and Criseyde*, now in the Pierpont Morgan Library, was made for or given to Henry V while he was Prince of Wales (Plate IX). In this same regard, learned men had long been sent to England as papal officials, and Humphrey must have known some of them. In any case, he had the idea of employing an Italian humanist as his secretary, which meant that he wanted to support a scholar who would do translations for him and dedicate them to him, from which he hoped to derive prestige as well as the pleasure of adding books to his library. The post was held successively by Tito Livio Frulovisi and Antonio Beccaria, but neither remained long in England. Italian scholars generally looked down on the English and regarded them as less generous than their own princes. Humphrey also employed scholars in Italy to prepare Latin translations of Greek classics and to find rare books for his library. In the 1430s and 1440s he was the center of a humanistic circle associated with Oxford, and he was the owner of a large and sophisticated library featuring classical books, many prepared by his own scholars and scribes. These procedures were not innovations, but methods already used by Richard de Bury and presumably the custom in Chaucer's time.

The gift of many books from Duke Humphrey's library was an enrichment to the intellectual advancement of Oxford and a precedent which other bibliophiles were not slow to follow. The benefits were reaped by young men soon to become the next generation of English humanists, some going to Italy after taking their degrees, not only to study at the universities, but also to visit the schools of humanist scholars, the most famous being that of Guarino da Verona, at Ferrara. Among Guarino's pupils was John Tiptoft, earl of Worcester (1427-72), who was to become, after Duke Humphrey, the greatest English bibliophile of the time.[54]

Tiptoft has been called the first Italianate Englishman. A Yorkist by family, he had the good fortune to be sent abroad by Henry VI during the Wars of the Roses, and he made no haste to return home, spending some years studying at Padua and at the school of Guarino. He certainly went to Florence, for he bought books from Vespasiano da Bisticci. By the time he returned to England he was the owner of a fine library. He soon became a powerful figure in English politics, serving as constable of England during the absence of Edward IV. He evidently took his position in the manner of an Italian prince, for his expedient justice earned him a bad reputation for executions, and he was himself condemned to death in 1472, at the age of 44.

Tiptoft admired Duke Humphrey, and his own will matched the generosity of his predecessor in behalf of Oxford, although the books went instead to Cambridge. Unlike Humphrey, however, he did considerable writing, which was much admired at the time. Caxton certainly thought well of him, for he printed his translations of Cicero's *De Amicitia* and of Buonaccorso de Montemagno's *Controversia de Nobilitate*, together with a preface which is highly complimentary to Tiptoft, even though the earl was dead when it appeared. While there is no evidence that Caxton had actually met Tiptoft, the fact of publication connects the printer with an important figure in early English humanism, who was also the most important English collector of books at the time. There were other notable personalities in Tiptoft's circle who were bibliophiles, such as John Free, Robert Flemmyng, dean of Lincoln, and William Grey, bishop of Ely.

While it is an assumption, and not a matter of record, that these owners of important private libraries possessed copies of works by so eminent an English poet as Chaucer, the manuscripts themselves frequently contain names of persons who owned them at various times. Although these persons cannot always be identified, and although the earliest history of the Chaucer manuscripts cannot be written for lack of information—especially the all-important information about their origins—there are enough records to show that, in addition to aristocrats, such prosperous urban families as the Pastons owned copies of works by Chaucer.

It remains to inquire what may have been the custom of fourteenth- and fifteenth-century collectors of books with regard to the furnishings of their libraries. Clark prints a fragment from a

👄 *Book Trade and Libraries*

cost book of Charles V of France listing expenses involved in fitting a tower of the Louvre to house the king's books (1367-68). The descriptions mention *bancs*, which could have been either presses or benches; *roes*, which were wheels; and *lettrins*, desks.[55] The wheels are an interesting development, not only in library equipment, but in the history of furniture, for there was far less interest in furniture in that day than one would suppose on the basis of present-day ideas of necessity and comfort. These wheels were revolving desks, consisting of a base, a central screw, and a revolving, polygonal lectern, which could be shared by several readers at once, seated upon benches. Small circular wheel desks, sometimes provided with a central spike for a candle or with an arm for a lantern, are often found in fifteenth-century art, which tends to show the reader seated behind this circular reading table in a heavy armchair. Besides the wheel table, illustrations show lectern-type reading stands, often massive and rigid, but sometimes adjustable by means of an angled screw in the bottom.

Since Chaucer's bookish persona claims to have been a bedtime reader, it is interesting to speculate whether the poet himself kept one of these wheel desks at his bed's head. In any event one had better not conjure up an Ellesmere-size volume balanced upon the ribs of a recumbent Chaucer. How the poet kept his own books, and the particular list he may have owned, there is no evidence to tell, but of his personal love for books there can be no doubt. With the seriousness that can lie behind laughter, he has the Eagle in the *House of Fame* accuse his persona of his eremitical life (652-60):

> For when thy labour doon al ys,
> And hast mad alle thy reckenynges,
> In stede of reste and newe thynges,
> Thou goost hom to thy hous anoon;
> And, also domb as any stoon,
> Thou sittest at another book
> Tyl fully daswed ys thy look,
> And lyvest thus as an hermyte,
> Although thyn abstynence ys lyte.

NOTES TO CHAPTER 4

¹The authoritative work on the subject is Wilhelm Wattenbach, *Das Schriftwesen im Mittelalter*, 3rd ed. (Leipzig, 1896).

²See above, p. 59.

³For discussion of fairs, see William Addison, *English Fairs and Markets* (London, 1953).

⁴James E. Thorold Rogers, *Six Centuries of Work and Wages* (London, 1909), pp. 149-52.

⁵The standard work on the subject is Jean Destrez, *La Pecia dans les manuscrits universitaires du XIIIe et du XIVe siècle* (Paris, 1935).

⁶"The Price of Books in Medieval England," *The Library*, 4th Ser., 17 (1937), 320. For discussion of wages and prices, to which there will be frequent reference in this chapter, see below, pp. 140-54.

⁷Bell, pp. 315-16.

⁸*La Pecia*, p. 74.

⁹Ibid., p. 36.

¹⁰George Gordon Coulton, *Chaucer and his England*, 8th ed. (1950; rpt. London, 1963). It is not clear whether Coulton believes this himself. See also Wilbur Lang Schramm, "The Cost of Books in Chaucer's Time," *MLN*, 48 (1933), 145.

¹¹Frank Arthur Mumby, *Publishing and Bookselling*, 4th ed. (London, 1949), p. 35.

¹²"The Extent of Literacy in England in the Fifteenth and Sixteenth Centuries: Notes and Conjectures," *The Library*, 4th Ser., 10 (1929-30), 163-93. See also Curt Ferdinand Bühler, *The Fifteenth-Century Book* (Philadelphia, 1960), pp. 42-44.

¹³"Vernacular Books in England in the Fourteenth and Fifteenth Centuries," *MLR*, 15 (1920), 349-58.

¹⁴Laura Hibbard Loomis, "The Auchinleck Manuscript and a Possible London Bookshop of 1330-1340," *PMLA*, 57 (1942), 595-627. See also "Sir Thopas," in *Sources and Analogues of Chaucer's "Canterbury Tales,"* ed. William Frank Bryan and Germaine Dempster (Chicago, 1941), pp. 486-559.

¹⁵See above, 4. See also Richard William Hunt, *et al.*, "Palaeography," in *Chambers's Encyclopaedia*, new ed. rev. (Oxford, 1967), X, 377-83.

¹⁶A. I. Doyle, "More Light on John Shirley," *Medium Aevum*, 30 (1961), 93-101. The projected continuation has not appeared.

◆§ *Book Trade and Libraries*

[17] Henry Stanley Bennett, *Chaucer and the Fifteenth Century* (Oxford, 1947), p. 118.

[18] Aage Brusendorff, *The Chaucer Tradition* (London, 1925), pp. 31-43. For Thomas Chaucer, see pp. 31-37. See also Martin Michael Crow and Clair Colby Olson, eds., *Chaucer Life Records* (Oxford, 1966), pp. 541-45.

[19] Graham Pollard, "The Company of Stationers Before 1557," *The Library*, 4th Ser., 18 (1937-38), 5-9.

[20] Bell, "Price of Books," p. 314.

[21] See above, p. 91.

[22] Bell, p. 316.

[23] For discussion see Beverly Boyd, *Chaucer and the Liturgy* (Philadelphia, 1968), p. 65.

[24] Bell, "Price of Books," pp. 314, 318, 321; see above, p. 24.

[25] Ibid., p. 328.

[26] Ibid.

[27] Ibid., p. 329.

[28] Ibid, p. 328.

[29] Ibid., pp. 329-30.

[30] "King Richard II's Books," *The Library*, 4th Ser., 13 (1932-33), 144-45.

[31] *Philobiblon*, ed. and trans. Ernest Chester Thomas (Oxford, 1960), p. 85.

[32] See below, p. 124.

[33] For these and other booksellers of the period, see Edward Gordon Duff, *A Century of the English Book Trade* (London, 1905).

[34] Mumby, *Publishing and Bookselling*, p. 43.

[35] Bühler, *The Fifteenth-Century Book*, p. 39. See also Henry Stanley Bennett, *English Books & Readers 1475-1557*, 2nd ed. (Cambridge, 1969), pp. 229-34.

[36] George Haven Putnam, *Books and Their Makers During the Middle Ages*, 2nd ed. (1898; rpt. New York, 1962), II, 124-25.

[37] Authoritative works on early libraries are John Willis Clark, *The Care of Books*, 2nd ed. (Cambridge, 1909); James Westphall Thompson, *The Medieval Library* (Chicago, 1939); Francis Wormald and Cyril E. Wright, eds., *The English Library Before 1700* (London, 1958); Neil Ripley Ker, *Medieval Libraries of Great Britain: A List of Surviving Books*, 2nd ed. (London, 1964).

38Francis Aidan [Cardinal] Gasquet, trans. *The Rule of St. Benedict* (London, 1925), pp. 84-87.

39Clark, *Care of Books*, pp. 58-59.

40Ibid., p. 68.

41Ibid.

42Ibid., p. 96.

43Strickland Gibson, "Printed Books, the Book-Trade, and Libraries," in Austin Lane Poole, ed., *Medieval England*, rev. ed. (Oxford, 1958), II, 566.

44Clark, p. 187.

45Ibid., pp. 145-53. See also Burnett Hillman Streeter, *The Chained Library* (London, 1931).

46Clark, *Care of Books*, pp. 161-62.

47Ibid., pp. 138-39.

48Ibid., pp. 100-02; 137; 116-17.

49"Chaucer and the Visconti Libraries," *ELH*, 6 (1939), 191-99.

50Edith Rickert, "Chaucer at School," *MP*, 29 (1932), 257-74; "Was Chaucer a Student at the Inner Temple?" *Manly Anniversary Studies in Language and Literature* (Chicago, 1923), pp. 20-31.

51Rickert, "Chaucer at School." The bequests are in two documents of St. Paul's Cathedral Library bound together in 1358: MS. A 67/46.

52Roberto Weiss, *Humanism in England During the Fifteenth Century* (Oxford, 1941).

53Kenneth Hotham Vickers, *Humphrey, Duke of Gloucester* (London, 1907).

54Rosamond Jocelyn Mitchell, *John Tiptoft (1427-1470)* (London, 1938).

55Clark, *Care of Books*, p. 294. See also p. 295, Fig. 139.

5

Chaucer, Published and Printed

THESE DISCUSSIONS have assumed an important fact about books: namely, publication. This term is now used very loosely, and will be so used in the present study, to mean the appearance of a book upon the market, and all the processes involved in that circumstance. But publication did not mean quite this in Chaucer's time. It referred to the official presentation of a finished work to some person, frequently to one who was rich and influential. That person was afterwards free to give copies to others.[1]

Publication under this system involved patronage, which was the source of an author's profit. Patronage was the normal way for an artist to practice his profession in the Middle Ages and earlier; Virgil had worked under patronage, as had the Anglo-Saxon scops and the French troubadours. Only the artist-monk had the security of an institution behind him, but he was at the mercy of his abbot. Either way, the system had the obvious disadvantage of depriving the artist of the freedom to do and say as he pleased—if, that is, he wished to keep his benefactors.

It is therefore not surprising that Chaucer, as a court poet, reveals at every turn diplomacy of kinds other than the foreign embassies which were part of his career. Although he was connected with some of the most powerful and controversial figures of the time, his writings and his life records are free from signs of conflict with any of them.[2] Such major socio-political matters as the Peasants' Revolt, the Wycliffite issue, and the deposition of Richard II appear in his works obliquely if at all.

Chaucer's financial profit from his career as a poet is more accurately measured in terms of the various government posts he held than in terms of outright grants. These posts, such as that of Controller of Customs and Subsidy on Wool, Skins, and Hides in the Port of London (1374-86), and that of Clerk of the King's Works, to which he acceded in 1389, were administrative positions. While such positions carried stipends, it is well known that persons who collected taxes had claim to a share of the revenues, and that benefits which would now be illegal accrued quite legally to persons holding government posts. Richard de Bury states openly that he took gifts in the form of books while he was chancellor of England.[3]

Official publication in the Middle Ages was more for the purpose of establishing credit with influential persons who could advance an author's career, as well as pay him a subsidy, than for dissemination of books to the public, although that was expected to follow. Publication, in fact, was not something authors rushed to achieve. The letters of Petrarch and Boccaccio show that official publication followed a long process of revising, during which an author might show, lend, or give copies of his project to others to obtain reaction, and even advance reputation, for a work still in progress. Needless to say, plagiarism was a constant threat. Both Petrarch and Boccaccio had work stolen and disseminated without their consent.[4]

When and if an author was ready to do so, he had a presentation copy prepared for his patron. He ceased to be in control of his work once this had been delivered, which explains why authors sometimes refused to publish. Petrarch, for example, never consented to the publication of his *Africa*. In two of his letters he refuses to show it and in a letter of 1363 he writes that he had once allowed a friend to copy thirty-four lines, but that the friend had broken a promise and permitted others to copy it, which they had done inaccurately.[5] Fear of incorrect copying also troubled Chaucer, for he writes at the end of *Troilus and Criseyde* (V, 1793-96),

> And for ther is so gret diversite
> In Englissh and in writyng of oure tonge,
> So prey I God that non myswrite the,
> Ne the mysmetre for defaute of tonge.

Since Chaucer was a famous poet in his own lifetime, the fact that he did not actually finish very much that he wrote raises an interesting question. Why, in that case, was he famous? One would suppose that the *Book of the Duchess* was presented, presumably to John of Gaunt, and it is probable that *Troilus and Criseyde* reached official publication, though scholars have been slow to accept the penultimate stanza, its rhetoric typical of dedications, as Chaucer's disposition of his book (V, 1856-59):

> O moral Gower, this book I directe
> To the and to the, philosophical Strode,
> To vouchen sauf, ther nede is, to correcte,
> Of youre benignites and zeles goode.

Apart from these polished works, and from the *Parliament of Fowls* and *Boece*, Chaucer's store of unfinished works is very large for a poet of his reputation.

Two explanations suggest themselves. First, strong internal evidence shows that he anticipated a listening public.[6] His works may have become famous because he read them before live audiences, which is what he is evidently doing in the miniature of the Cambridge *Troilus* (Plate VI).[7] Thus he was under no particular pressure to finish things to a state of polish for official presentation. A second possibility is that, besides reading from his works, especially the *Canterbury Tales*, he gave, or even officially presented, finished items to people he knew, even though he had plans for uniting the individual pieces into the larger work. Evidence of this resides in the little poem addressed to Bukton. Chaucer recommends (29-30) "The Wyf of Bathe I pray yow that ye rede / Of this matere that we have on honde." The matter at hand is, of course, marriage. Bukton could hardly have read the

Wife of Bath unless he had a copy. Certainly, Chaucer must have placed his writings before a wider public than is indicated by the few works he finished, or he would not have achieved fame in his own lifetime.

At the time of Chaucer's death in 1400, a new figure entered the management of his literary works: the editor. As noted earlier, little is known about the editing and copying of the extant manuscripts, all of them posthumous, of any of Chaucer's writings.[8] If scholars had more information about John Shirley and his atelier, and more about those responsible for the earliest extant Chaucer manuscripts, William Caxton's role as the poet's first known major editor and publisher, as well as his first printer, would not seem so innovative as it now appears.[9] But this circumstance is not likely to change very much now, and such change would not, in any case, alter the fact that Caxton is a titan, whereas these other men are scarcely known. It is perhaps unfortunate that his importance as Chaucer's first printer has come to overshadow the fact that he is the only fifteenth-century editor and copyist of Chaucer whose career and methods can be studied extensively. Although he operated a printing business, and although he was not originally either a scribe or a stationer, the material relating to Caxton is the best evidence there is of the workings of those who produced the Chaucer manuscripts in the fifteenth century. For, as already observed, those who printed books this early were not seeking to revolutionize the idea of a book; they intended their copies to be as much like other books as possible. By the time of his death *ca.* 1491, Caxton had put out editions of the following works by Chaucer:

Anelida and Arcite, with "The Complaint of Chaucer to his Purse:" 1477.
The Parliament of Fowls (then known as *The Temple of Brass*), with "Truth" (also known as "Balade de Bon Conseyl"), "Lenvoy de Chaucer a Skogan," and "Fortune" (also known as "Balades de Visage sanz Peinture"): 1477.
Canterbury Tales, first edition: 1478 (Plate X).
Boece: 1478.

Chaucer, Published and Printed

Troilus and Criseyde: 1484.
Canterbury Tales, second edition: 1484 (Plate XI).
The House of Fame (then known as *The Book of Fame*): 1484.[10]

It is impossible to understand Caxton's operations as a printer and editor—as a scribe of Chaucer who had a machine to do the actual work of copying—without knowing something of his life and career. While very little can be deduced about his family background, and while even the date of his birth has to be inferred from other evidence, there is every indication that he came of a prosperous family, and that he had had some education before being apprenticed (1438) to an important London mercer who was at one time Lord Mayor. He afterwards became associated with the Merchants Adventurers, an organization of overseas guildsmen, chiefly mercers, based primarily in Bruges, then part of Burgundy. He became governor of this important institution in 1462 or 1463, the date being indeterminate since custom varied with regard to the location of New Year's Day on the calendar. Caxton evidently reckoned dates from Easter, as was the custom in Belgium.

As governor of the Merchants Adventurers, Caxton held a position that was very important politically, in an environment which could not have failed to enrich a man who loved books, for Bruges, besides being an international city filled with people involved in foreign trade, was also a center of the book arts. The dukes of Burgundy had one of the largest libraries in Europe, said to have numbered two thousand volumes. Most recent opinion holds that the mercers traded in other goods besides textiles, and that importing books from Bruges was a major aspect of their business.[11]

The Merchants Adventurers served as a link between the English monarchy and the Burgundian court at a time when trade relations were often tense. The fact that England was at war, first with the French and then within itself, meant that the governor of the Merchants Adventurers was one of the most important Englishmen in Europe. Caxton took part in a number of highly sensitive diplomatic negotiations during the Wars of the Roses, including that which resulted in the marriage of Charles of Burgundy to Margaret of York, sister of Edward IV, in 1468. In the course of these negotiations he met many important people, including aristocrats who were later to become his patrons. Not least among these was Margaret herself, for it was she who encouraged him to write.

It is not known how or when Caxton became seriously interested in literature. At some point before the end of 1468, however, he had read *Le Recueil des histoires de Troyes*, by Raoul Le Fevre, secretary to Philip, the previous duke of Burgundy.[12] This work, a French translation of earlier accounts of the Trojan War, must have impressed Caxton greatly, for he had the idea of translating it into English. His own claim that he did so to avoid sloth and idleness is probably as much a true projection of his ever-busy personality as the exaggeration of contemporary rhetoric so often assumed. In any case, he states in the prologue he afterwards wrote for his printed edition that he had given up after a few quires, and that the duchess had commanded him to finish it, which he had done at Cologne in 1471.[13]

Caxton's motives may have been precisely as described, but they cannot have been unrelated to other developments. First of all, he ceased to be governor of the Merchants Adventurers at this time or slightly earlier, for no recorded reason. Secondly, authorities are now largely in agreement that he learned to print, also in Cologne, at about the same time.[14] While it is no longer believed that he left his position in order to enter Margaret's service, or indeed that he was ever a member of her household, it can hardly be coincidental that translation was then a fashion in English literature, and that printing had business possibilities along lines that had not yet been explored.

Caxton's own account of his venture into printing is probably true, but not the whole truth. According to him, once his book had been presented to the Duchess he was beset with requests for copies, which he could not fill because of the slowness of the process of copying and the difficulty of the effort, which he seems

◈❥ *Chaucer, Published and Printed*

to have undertaken himself. He says in the Epilogue to Book III of his printed edition,

> And for as moche as in the wrytyng of the same my penne is worn, myn hande wery *and* not stedfast, myn eyen di*m*med with overmoche lokyng on the whit paper, and my corage not so prone and redy to laboure as hit hath ben, and that age crepeth on me dayly and febleth all the bodye, and also be cause I have promysid to dyverce gentilmen and to my frendes to adresse to hem as hastely as I myght this sayd book: Therfore I have practysed *and* lerned at my grete charge and dispense to ordeyne this said book in prynte after the maner *and* forme as ye may here see....[15]

That he should have insisted upon learning to print, and at his own expense, instead of employing someone for the purpose makes little sense unless he intended to become a professional. In any case, the book, known as *The Recuyell of the hystoryes of Troye*, was printed at Bruges in 1473 or 1474, and Caxton claims to have done the work himself. This is, of course, the first book printed in English.[16]

The press at Bruges involved some sort of partnership with the printer Colard Mansion, who had previously been a scribe and bookseller.[17] It was formerly thought that Mansion, himself an excellent printer, had taught Caxton the new art. While this is no longer believed, it cannot be unimportant that Mansion had as one of his patrons Louis de Bruges, a noted bibliophile who had risen to political prominence by giving hospitality to Edward IV during his flight from the Lancastrians, for which service he had been created Earl of Winchester. Caxton evidently thought a successful printing business could be worked with such backing as he and Mansion had between them. From this press came the following books during their association:

1. *The Recuyell of the hystoryes of Troye*, translated and printed by Caxton, with prologue and epilogues.
2. *Le Recueil des histoires de Troyes*, by Raoul Le Fevre.

3. *The game and playe of the chesse*, first edition, translated by Caxton with prologue; Latin original by Jacobus de Cessolis, translated into French by Jehan de Vignay.
4. *Les fais et proesses du noble et vaillant chevalier Jason*, by Raoul Le Fevre.
5. *Meditacions sur les sept pseaumes penitenciaulx*, by Pierre d'Ailly.[18]

Caxton's personal role in any of these but the first and third is doubtful; he may not actually have printed the third.

The type used for these books printed at the Bruges press produced a page very closely resembling the page of a manuscript.[19] Its punctuation is rudimentary: comma (/), colon, and period. Scholars have long believed that it was made by John Veldener of Louvain. It was a bastard version of the Secretary book hand of the time and place, possibly modeled upon Mansion's own writing. Precisely how the type was produced has to be concluded from later sources, for there are no contemporary treatises on typefounding, but it is thought to have been cast by some method involving the three-step procedure typical of the earliest descriptions of typecasting:

1. The letter was cut in relief upon a piece of hard metal, producing a *punch*.
2. The punch was struck into a piece of softer metal, producing a *matrix*.
3. The matrix was placed in the bottom of a laterally adjustable mold into which molten metal was poured, presumably some alloy of lead and antimony.

The shank (body) of the type was the key to the whole process of printing with movable type, for when the types were assembled, they were supposed to fit together so precisely that they could be locked into one rigid whole (form) by means of a frame resembling a bottomless box (chase), which presented the faces of the type, cut in relief, in a printing surface which was perfectly flat.[20] The first and still authoritative study of Caxton's typog-

Chaucer, Published and Printed

raphy is that of William Blades. Blades found that Caxton had used a total of eight castings (fonts) of type, which he listed as follows: 1, 2, 2*, 3, 4, 4*, 5, 6. Starred castings were revisions of the preceding font. To this series, numbers seven and eight have since been added. The books listed above which were printed at the Bruges press are all in the type now called Caxton's Type No. 1.

There are no contemporary descriptions of fifteenth-century printing presses. Scholars have learned about them from books that were printed at the time, from pictorial representations, and from later treatises on printing. Early presses were wooden structures, their principles traceable to those of Roman wine and olive presses, as well as to presses used to remove moisture from newly-made paper. They consisted of a structure formed by two uprights joined by two horizontal beams. In the upper beam there was a screw, turned by a lever. This exerted pressure on a wooden plank placed on the paper which was to receive the printed impression. The twisting movement of the screw was counteracted by suspending the wooden plank (platen) from a hollow wooden box (hose) that slid inside closely fitting guides while the screw turned freely inside. From the front of the press projected a plank, supported by a prop. Upon this plank were rails. A slab of wood (carriage) was mounted on these rails. Upon the carriage was placed a rectangular frame (coffin) which contained a flat piece of marble or limestone. The chase containing the form of type was laid on the stone. To the end of the carriage farthest from the platen was hinged another frame, tightly covered with parchment (tympan). The tympan bore the paper for printing, which was attached to it by projecting points. To the tympan was hinged a light hinged frame (frisket). When the type had been inked, the frisket was closed down over the tympan containing dampened paper. Both were then closed down over the chase containing the inked form of type. The carriage was then moved by means of a windlass (rounce) until the chase was in position under the platen.

The physical work of printing was done by two men, one to

pull the lever which turned the screw lowering and raising the platen, and one to work the ink, which was applied by beating with leather balls stuffed with wool. The press in Gutenberg's time must have been more primitive, but it cannot have been much different in principle. According to recent opinion, the most important difference between the first presses and those increasingly in use in Caxton's time was the addition of the carriage. Fifteenth-century printers produced from the form single printed sheets (broadsides), used mainly for notices, and pages typical of manuscript books of the time, chiefly folio and quarto. Since the platen was only half as large as a typical form of type containing two folio pages, it required two pulls of the press to print the entire form. The invention of the carriage greatly speeded the process of printing, for, having printed one half of the form, the pressman could pull the lever raising the platen, crank the carriage so that the rest of the form was in position under the platen, and then make his second impression. This was easier and quicker than the original system by which the form had to be removed and inked each time one folio page was printed.[21]

Returning to Caxton: if he had not already decided to move to England, the political tides of the year 1476 might have persuaded him to do so. Burgundy was defeated in that year at the Battle of Morat, and Charles was slain in June at Nanci. Margaret retired to Malines. Edward IV, on the other hand, appeared at the moment firmly established in England. As for Caxton's association with Colard Mansion, the fact that Mansion eventually became insolvent and disappeared from history raises many questions about the financing of the Bruges press.

Why Caxton selected Westminster as the location of his new press may have many explanations, but the old theory that he was avoiding conflict with the London guilds seems less likely than N. F. Blake's belief that he was at first seeking an aristocratic market, to which Westminster would have been convenient.[22] From the size of his total output in the seventeen years of his career as a printer, numbering over one hundred items including those more in the nature of pamphlets than of books, it is ob-

Chaucer, Published and Printed

vious that Caxton, who was not a young man, could not have done all the physical work of printing as well as the great labor of editing and translating. Instead, his position must have been that of an administrator. Others did the actual work of printing while he did the preparation of the books that came from his press. This is certainly more in keeping with his previous career in the Merchants Adventurers. That Wynkyn de Worde came with him from Bruges, or even from Cologne as some have thought, is uncertain, but the fact that he inherited Caxton's business proves that he had a hand in much of the work produced at Westminster. He is thought to have been Caxton's foreman.[23] It was Richard Pynson, not Wynkyn de Worde, who first took up the printing of the *Canterbury Tales* after Caxton's death, Wynkyn's operation of the business he had inherited having been delayed by litigation. Although Pynson's edition (1492) is a reprint of Caxton's second edition, he is not known to have been connected with Caxton's shop.[24]

Caxton had brought from Bruges a new type, now called Type No. 2, from which only one book had been printed before, a French translation of a Latin book of meditations, known as *Cordiale*.[25] Veldener is thought to have been once again the typefounder. Needless to say, Type No. 2 is that of the earliest books printed at Westminster, including the early Chaucers. Also modeled upon a Flemish Bastard Secretary script, its chief characteristic is the irregular size and shape of its capitals, which gives the type an appearance which Blades has called "dashing" (Plate X).[26]

The first publications from Caxton's new press were not books, properly speaking, but pamphlets, among which is a quarto edition of ten leaves containing Chaucer's *Anelida and Arcite* and his "Complaint to his Purse."[27] Why Caxton printed the two together is anyone's guess: he may have found them that way in his source, or he may have hoped that Chaucer's message to Henry IV in the "Complaint" might also do him some good financially, since Henry had rewarded Chaucer with a stipend. He obviously printed short works by important authors because he felt obliged to make his presence known to his future patrons while he worked on something more substantial. The same is undoubtedly true of the little miscellany that contains, among other pieces, *The Parliament of Fowls*, "Truth," and "Lenvoy de Chaucer a Skogan." Both were printed *ca.* 1477.[28]

The first real books Caxton printed at Westminster are associated with the patronage of Anthony Woodville, Earl Rivers, whom he had presumably met in Bruges. Rivers was the Queen's brother, and tutor to the Prince of Wales, who was then seven. In 1477, Caxton printed *The Dictes or Sayengis of the philosophres*, a translation by Rivers, who says in the preface that he had read the original in French during a pilgrimage to Compostella, and that he had translated it for the Prince.[29] Caxton also printed at about the same time one of his own translations, *The History of Jason*, which had been printed in French at the Bruges press from the version by Raoul Le Fevre.[30] This book was also presented to the Prince. The Woodvilles remained Caxton's most important patrons until the death of Edward IV. Their role, and the roles other patrons played in Caxton's career, show that he had in mind for his books the same kind of clientele as the audience for whom Chaucer had written.

That many, if not most, of the books Caxton printed were produced under patronage is clear from his prefaces. He may have principally wanted the names of important aristocrats, who themselves gained honor from the association with culture and learning, to lend prestige to his books. Someone in any case had to underwrite these ventures with either subsidies or promises to buy in quantity. That Caxton was able to keep himself supplied with capital is borne out by the fact that his shop, which may have bought and sold other books besides his own, became and remained successful, a story that is not true of most other fifteenth-century printers. Nor were aristocrats the only persons whose backing Caxton sought. He constantly implies friendship with important, and presumably wealthy, merchants, whom he naturally knew through his own connections as a mercer, and the *Boece* was printed "atte requeste of a singuler frende & gossib of

~§ Chaucer, Published and Printed

myne," whom Blake identifies as the London mercer, William Pratt.[31] *The book callid Caton*, translated from the French and produced in 1483, is dedicated to the City of London.[32]

Caxton seems to have had several basic procedures for deciding what to print. First of all, there were books, such as his *Recuyell*, which he wanted to issue, presumably because they were works he liked himself and knew he could sell. Evidently he underwrote these by interesting prospective patrons. But he also printed by arrangement with persons who either wanted him to reproduce a favorite book or who had a book he himself wished to print. In such cases, he seems to have viewed his role as a business transaction, not as a scholarly endeavor. This happens to be one of the most important facts in the history of Chaucer's works, for Caxton printed the first edition of the *Canterbury Tales* under some such arrangement *ca.* 1478, only to discover later that he had printed from a poor source. He tells the story himself in the preface he wrote for the second edition (*ca.* 1484):

> I purpose temprynte by the grace of god the book of the tales of cauntyrburye, in whiche I fynde many a noble hystorye, of every astate and degre: Fyrst rehercyng the condicions, and tharraye of eche of them as properly as possyble is to be sayd: And after theyr tales whyche ben of noblesse, wysedom, gentylesse, Myrthe, and also of veray holynesse and vertue, wherin he fynysshyth thys sayd booke, whyche book I have dylygently oversen and duly examyned to thende that it be made acordyng unto his owen makyng: For I fynde many of the sayd bookes, whyche wryters have abrydgyd it and many thynges left out, And in somme place have sette certayn versys, that he never made ne sette in hys booke, of whyche bookes so incorrecte was one brought to me vj yere passyd, whyche I supposed had ben veray true *and* correcte: And accordyng to the same I dyde do enprynte a certayn nombre of them, whyche anon were sold to many and dyverse gentyl men, of whome one gentylman cam to me, and said that this book was not accordyng in many places unto the book that Gefferey chaucer had made: To whom I answerd that I had made it accordyng to my copye, and by me was nothyng added ne

Chaucer and the Medieval Book

mynusshyd: Thenne he sayd he knewe a book whyche hys fader had and moche lovyd, that was very trewe, and accordyng unto hys owen first book by hym made, and sayd more yf I wold enprynte it agayn he wold gete me the same book for a copye, how be it he wyst wel, that hys fader wold not gladly departe fro it: To whom I said, in caas that he coude gete me suche a book trewe and correcte, yet I wold ones endevoyre me to enprynte it agayn, for to satysfye thauctour, where as to fore by ygnouraunce I erryd in hurtyng and dyffamyng his book in dyverce places in settyng in somme thynges that he never sayd ne made, and levyng out many thynges that he made whyche ben requysite to be sette in it: And thus we fyll at accord: And he ful gentylly gate of hys fader the said book, and delyverd it to me, by whiche I have corrected my book, as here after alle alonge by thayde of almyghty god shal folowe, whom I humbly beseche to gyve me grace and ayde to achyeve, and accomplysshe, to hys laude honour and glorye, and that alle ye that shal in thys book rede or heere, wyll of your charyte emong your dedes of mercy, remembre the sowle of the sayd Gefferey chaucer first auctour, and ma ker of thys book: And also that alle we that shal see and rede therin, may so take and understonde the good and vertuous tales, that it may so prouffyte, unto the helthe of our sowles, that after thys short and transitorye lyf we may come to everlastyng lyf in heven: Amen[33]

Caxton's apology has been judged in largely commercial terms by Blake, who sees in it an excuse to bring out another edition of a book that had already sold well.[34] But this is judging the printer harshly, for the faults of the first edition are exactly as described, and it did his reputation no good to become known for poor work. It is here assumed that the apology is sincere and that it is to be taken literally. Caxton insists that the shortcomings of the first edition are no fault of his own, since the manuscript source had been brought to him, and since he had taken pains to follow his copy. Having inadvertently done injury to a great poet by printing from a poor manuscript, he owed Chaucer the reparation of putting out a better edition. It must be admitted, however, that there are signs of haste in all Caxton's work. He did not investi-

~§ *Chaucer, Published and Printed*

gate his sources before he printed, especially when work was brought to him by others for printing. Although he was a capable scholar, his career as a printer is the story of a man in a hurry.

Caxton's second edition of the *Canterbury Tales* is not a new transcription. Instead, as he says in the preface, the printer corrected the old edition from the new manuscript. That he proceeded in this way is another sign of haste. But there were conditioning factors. In the first place, the owner had been reluctant to lend the manuscript, and Caxton may have been obliged to work very rapidly in order to return it. The particular reason may have been that it was a luxury copy. Although there are no woodcuts in the first edition, it must be remembered that Caxton was not using woodcuts that early. The twenty-three in the second edition were probably taken from Caxton's new source. But with a valuable book as his master copy, he would not have risked any damage or marks, and a new transcription would have been difficult to prepare and would have taken a long time. Caxton's procedure may not have been ideal, but it was practical.

The reaction to the first edition which Caxton describes is justified. He lists two complaints: omissions, and insertions of lines which are not genuine. To this should be added alterations of lines. The total differences are analyzed in full by Thomas C. Dunn.[35] Whoever inserted the spurious lines had made a deliberate attempt to be bawdy. The fact that Caxton's client (or perhaps he was a patron) understood Chaucer's style well enough to know that the lines in question were not genuine is particularly interesting in terms of the chaotic state of the manuscripts, a matter of which Caxton must have been ignorant when he printed the first edition. There is, of course, no way of knowing on what authority the owner of the new manuscript believed his copy to be authentic. The first source-manuscript cannot have been a mere maverick, for Manly and Rickert found that, excluding links from their consideration, Caxton's first edition follows the order of Group *b*, one of the four major groups of manuscripts classified by order of the tales. Even more importantly, in other matters it belongs to Group b̰ of their textual classification.[36]

Since Caxton claims that he had followed his source carefully in printing his first edition and that its faults are not any error of his own, it seems unlikely that he would have made any major changes in the text as presented by the new manuscript, which, as he says himself, was believed by its owners to be "very trewe, and accordyng unto hys [Chaucer's] owen first book by hym made."

The orders of the tales given by the two editions differ. They are:

C^1: A B^1 F^1 E^2 D E^1 F^2 G C B^2 H I
C^2: A B^1 E^2 F D E^1 G C B^2 H I

Since a formula alone is of little use to anyone not already expert in textual matters, the *Canterbury Tales* are listed here in the Ellesmere order (that of Manly and Rickert's group *a*). The numbers of the fragments are accompanied by the letters which are used to represent the order of the tales which would be achieved by following the Bradshaw Shift, together with a relocation of Fragment VI once recommended by the Chaucer Society but no longer widely espoused.

Fragment I (Group A)
  General Prologue
  The Knight's Tale
  The Miller's Prologue and Tale
  The Reeve's Prologue and Tale
  The Cook's Prologue and Tale
Fragment II (Group B^1)
  The Man of Law's Introduction, Prologue, and Tale
Fragment III (Group D)
  The Wife of Bath's Prologue and Tale
  The Friar's Prologue and Tale
  The Summoner's Prologue and Tale
Fragment IV (Group E)
  The Clerk's Prologue and Tale
  The Merchant's Prologue and Tale
Fragment V (Group F)
  The Squire's Introduction and Tale
  The Franklin's Prologue and Tale

⋑§ Chaucer, Published and Printed

Fragment VI (Group C)
  The Physician's Tale
  The Pardoner's Introduction, Prologue, and Tale
Fragment VII (Group B^2)
  The Shipman's Tale
  The Prioress's Prologue and Tale
  The Prologue and Tale of Sir Thopas
  The Prologue and Tale of Melibee
  The Monk's Prologue and Tale
  The Nun's Priest's Prologue and Tale
Fragment VIII (Group G)
  The Second Nun's Prologue and Tale
  The Canon's Yeoman's Prologue and Tale
Fragment IX (Group H)
  The Manciple's Prologue and Tale
Fragment X (Group I)
  The Parson's Prologue and Tale
  Chaucer's Retraction[37]

Caxton's second edition shows an order closer to Manly and Rickert's group *a*, but it is not a member of it. The most important difference in order between the first and second editions is the combination of F^1 and F^2. Dunn believes that Caxton made this change himself, and that he did so because his new source contained the words of the Franklin to the Squire that should form the link.[38] This may be true, but it does not agree with Caxton's stated purpose in putting out the corrected edition: namely, that the new copy was "very trewe, and accordyng unto his [Chaucer's] owen first book by hym made. . . ." Caxton would hardly have so described the new book if it had needed so radical a change. That he should have made this change and left so obvious a misplacement as the separation of the Clerk's tale and that of the Merchant, when he had the seven lines that link them, may not demolish Dunn's theory that Caxton made changes in the order of the tales, but it raises a serious objection. In any event, Caxton's new source, while known to have been a better one than that of his first edition, and in fact a very good manuscript, is not extant and his second edition is no longer an active source in textual criticism. It was, however, enormously important for a long time, since subsequent editions of the *Canterbury Tales* were based on this one for centuries.

That Caxton had a conscience in matters concerning his sources can also be seen in his edition of the *House of Fame*, printed in about the same year as the second edition of the *Canterbury Tales*. This work, however short, raises the question of editorial emendation, which scribes had long felt free to supply and which had already caused Caxton the embarrassment of repudiating the first edition of the *Canterbury Tales*. When he came to print the *House of Fame*, he realized that his source lacked a conclusion. He says in his epilogue,

> I fynde nomore of this werke to fore sayd: For as fer as I can understonde, This noble man Gefferey Chaucer fynysshyd at the sayd conclusion of the metyng of lesyng and sothsawe, where as yet they ben chekked and maye not departe, whyche werke as me semeth is craftyly made, and dygne to be wreton *and* knowen: For he towchyth in it ryght grete wysedom *and* subtyll understondyng: And so in alle hys werkys he excellyth in myn oppynyon alle other wryters in our Englyssh, For he wrytteth no voyde wordes, but alle hys mater is ful of hye and quycke sentence, to whom ought to be gyven laude and preysyng for hys noble makyng and wrytyng: For of hym alle other have borowed syth and taken, in alle theyr wel sayeng and wrytyng: And I humbly beseche *and* praye yow, emonge your prayers to remembre hys soule, on whyche and on alle crysten soulis I beseche almyghty god to have mercy: Amen.[39]

Nevertheless, Caxton saw fit to invent a conclusion himself. Since his source lacked lines of the unfinished poem that appear in the principal manuscripts, his patch follows line 2094:

> And wyth the noyse of them wo
> I sodeynly awoke anon tho
> And remembryd what I had seen
> And how hye and ferre I had been

> In my ghoost and had grete wonder
> Of that the god of thonder
> Had lete me knowen and began to wryte
> Lyke as ye have herd me endyte
> Wherfor to studye and rede alway
> I purpose to doo day by day
> Thus in dremyng and in game
> Endeth thys lytyl book of Fame.[40]

His own name is carefully placed in the margin next to his lines. Caxton must have seen emendation of whole lines and passages as correct procedure so long as it was properly acknowledged. His willingness to use it shows how close he was to contemporary scribal customs.

Caxton may have taken no more care to examine his source before printing Chaucer's other major poem, *Troilus and Criseyde*, than he had taken before printing the first edition of the *Canterbury Tales*. This edition was likewise based on a poor source, from which—or perhaps from the source of which—leaves were missing: notably at Book I, 449-504; II, 246-301; III, 114-69. On two occasions an eight-stanza leaf was reversed in the source, so that in Book I lines 785-812 follow line 959. Also, in Book III, lines 442-75, five stanzas are omitted. A number of lines and short passages show unique corruptions, which R. K. Root attributes to "conjectural emendation of Caxton's editing."[41] This criticism, however, must be read against Caxton's prefaces, for his own claims in dealing with Chaucer are to careful adherence to his source. As already seen, in *The House of Fame* he carefully acknowledges emendation. It is doubtful that Caxton would have been really careless in dealing with Chaucer once he had a text in hand, especially in the case of this tale of the Trojan War, which must have been a topic close to his own liking in view of his previous work with the *Recueil des histoires de Troyes*. It is more probable that the source is at fault, and that Caxton either did not investigate the copy before he printed it, or else obtained the best copy he could find, which happened to be a poor one.

The matter of text requires discussion. Chaucer's poem exists in twenty-one manuscripts, five being fragments.[42] One manuscript (MS. Phillipps 8250, privately owned), copied by a single scribe and unfortunately full of errors, represents what scholars believe to be the original version, which they call *alpha*. Root, in his study of the texts, identifies a revision, which he calls *beta*. Caxton's source represented the *beta* version. Indeed, his edition is the only copy which follows *beta* throughout, so that his edition, unlike his editions of the *Canterbury Tales*, is still valuable as an authoritative record of a particular text. While some manuscripts represent mixed sources, *alpha* and *beta*, there is still another version of the poem, which Root believes to represent *beta* before it was completed, and which he calls *gamma*. More recent opinion holds that *gamma* is the revision, and that *beta* is a text worked upon by someone other than Chaucer.[43] It is a fact that the best and most handsome manuscripts follow *gamma*, including the Campsall Manuscript, to which reference has already been made.[44] Caxton had certainly found a revised version of the poem, but not the right one, and not a good copy in the first place.

From Blake's critical essay on the subject of Caxton as an editor it is clear that the printer had one manner of dealing with poetry, especially with that by so famous an English author as Chaucer, and quite another manner of dealing with prose.[45] He was freer about making changes in the prose works he issued—provided that the author was not so celebrated and so recent as Chaucer, whose *Boece* he printed with few differences, all minor, *ca.* 1478[46]—or provided that the author was not one of his patrons. An amusing insight into Caxton on the horns of a textual and social dilemma (the more amusing because he has little other discernable humor) occurs in the preface he wrote for Rivers' *Dictes or Sayengis of the philosophres*, for he had found that Rivers had discretely left out a misogynistic passage attributed to Socrates. Since he could not well tamper with his patron's work, and since he was unable to persuade Rivers to restore the deleted passage, Caxton gave it an epilogue of his own, noting that Rivers must have been put up to the omission by some lady: in any case, he is giving the passage himself, since it does not apply to women of his own time and country.[47] This incident has an unintentionally serious dimension, for it leads one to expect that Caxton thought he took care to represent his texts accurately.

Returning to the subject of Caxton's type fonts, it will be remembered that Type No. 2 was brought to England when the new press was established, so that it was the type used for the earliest books printed at Westminster, including the Chaucers. Type No. 2 was presently revised, no doubt because some of the types were wearing out. It is not known whether Caxton did the work of recasting himself. The result is Type No. 2*, later used for the headings in the second edition of the *Canterbury Tales*. Caxton also had occasion to print Latin, and there was an especially good market for liturgical books. Early printers were still working under the traditions of calligraphy, and much that was written in Latin, especially liturgical books, required the most formal Gothic (Parkes calls it Textura) handwriting and therefore Gothic type. Caxton had a type for the purpose, Type No. 3, which Blake thinks he already had before he left Bruges,[48] although he sent his Sarum missal to be printed in France. *Boece* is printed in Type No. 2 save for the Latin epigraphs, which are in No. 3. Caxton did not print very much in this type, whether because he did not care for it or, more likely, because his specialty was vernacular books, for which type derived from Secretary hand was more appropriate.

Hitherto, Caxton had had no serious competition, since the second printer to open shop in England, the German Theodore Rood, had elected to work in Oxford, not London, and he appears to have had no interest in vernacular books. But in 1480, John Lettou appeared in London. As events proved, he was not going to compete for the same trade, either, but he was a better printer than Caxton. He worked in a small Gothic type and in double columns. There is little doubt that Caxton became conscious of the appearance of his pages at about this time, for he made some changes in his typography. He obtained a new font of type, which was smaller and neater (Type No. 4), and he began to use lines even at both margins when printing prose. In the 1481 edition of the *Mirrour of the World*, he also began to use woodcut illustrations.[49] It was in the revision of the new type, Type No. 4*, that Caxton issued the rest of his Chaucers, including the second edition of the *Canterbury Tales* and *Troilus and Criseyde*.

Some general and practical remarks about Caxton's books in terms of other incunabula are now appropriate. In the first place, although colophons at the ends of books had long been familiar, it was not yet customary to use title pages. Nor was it considered essential to make a point of announcing the facts of publication, so that incunabula are often without dates, which have to be deduced from other evidence, titles being known in several, if not many, versions. The first book printed in England with a title page is an edition of the *Book against the pestilence*, by Canutus, bishop of Westeraes (Sweden), printed by William de Machlinia at an unknown date before 1490. Although Caxton did not use title pages, Wynkyn de Worde began to do so soon after the printer's death. Once the title page had become a regular feature of printed books, the colophon became unnecessary and gradually went out of use except in special cases.[50]

As for pages themselves, the early printers first sorted their paper, as it was sometimes irregular. While fifteenth-century books usually have the same watermark throughout, there can be a variety of watermarks if the printer has used paper from different lots.[51] Printers from the beginning worked by forms.[52] At first they added signatures in ink at the bottoms of pages, and these were trimmed off during binding but Caxton and others began to print them close to the text after *ca.* 1480.

Capitals and other rubrication were originally added to incunabula by a specialist, the printer supplying only guide letters. Caxton was for some reason slow to employ woodcut initials and other woodcut art. Woodcut initials first appear in his *Aesop* (1484),[53] but he used them only for one year. They reappear permanently in 1487. As for his woodcut art, this has already been discussed in connection with other book art.[54] His best woodcut

Chaucer, Published and Printed

—or the best work of his woodcut artist whoever he may have been—is the frontispiece to his *Fifteen Oes* (*ca.* 1491).[55] There is no evidence that Caxton did this kind of work himself.

Caxton's importance to English history is the fact that he was the first Englishman to print in his own language and in his own country. His importance to literature is another matter. Here his contribution is the fact that he printed all the major English literature of the time which would have been acceptable in court circles, as well as other important, or at least timely, literature in English translation. He did this at a period when Englishmen were becoming increasingly aware of their own language and literature. Of original literature, he wrote none himself except a last book he composed for John Trevisa's English translation of Higden's *Polychronicon*, bringing it down to the date of its printing (1482),[56] and his own prologues and epilogues, which are vital to any understanding of the way he worked.

Wynkyn de Worde and Richard Pynson, both of whom reprinted *Canterbury Tales*, were Caxton's successors in the printing of works by Chaucer. Their publications are interesting to specialists in the history of typography but add nothing to the history of Chaucer's books except confirmation of the popularity of the *Canterbury Tales* in the 1490s. It remains to estimate what Caxton achieved by printing his Chaucers. From a textual point of view, he achieved nothing permanent. Although later editions were made from his for a long time to come and not from new transcriptions of the manuscripts, they do not perpetuate authoritative texts. On the other hand, he is the best available witness to the state of the Chaucer manuscripts in the late fifteenth century, to the conditions under which they were copied, and to the attitudes of copyists toward their sources. Bad texts circulated with good, and it may have been Caxton's issuance of identical copies which brought the fact to light in the first place. While Caxton was not a professional stationer before he turned to editing and translating books, his business sense made his press a success, and must have placed Chaucer's writings in numerous libraries. Thus it was Caxton, rather than the unknown editors of the Elles-

Chaucer and the Medieval Book

mere and Hengwrt manuscripts, who determined the form in which Chaucer's most beloved work, the *Canterbury Tales*, was known to the reading public for many generations.

NOTES TO CHAPTER 5

[1] For discussion, see Robert Kilburn Root, "Publication Before Printing," *PMLA*, 28 (1913), 417-31; see also Henry Stanley Bennett, "The Author and His Public in the Fourteenth and Fifteenth Centuries," *Essays and Studies by Members of the English Association*, 23 (1938), 7-24.

[2] See Martin Michael Crow and Clair Colby Olson, eds., *Chaucer Life-Records* (Oxford, 1966). For discussion of Chaucer's acquaintances, see George Williams, *A New View of Chaucer* (Durham, N.C., 1965).

[3] *Philobiblon*, ed. and trans. Ernest Chester Thomas (Oxford, 1960), p. 83.

[4] Root, "Publication Before Printing," pp. 420-21; Giuseppe Fracassetti, ed., *Epistolae de Rebus Familiaribus* (Florence, 1859-63); Giuseppe Corazzini, ed., *Le lettere edite ed inedite di Messer Giovanni Boccaccio* (Florence, 1877).

[5] Root, p. 420; *Epist. fam.*, 12, VII; 13, XI (Fracasetti, I, 185-87; II, 261-63).

[6] For discussion of Chaucer's listening public, see Ruth Crosby, "Oral Delivery in the Middle Ages," *Speculum*, 11 (1936), 88-110; "Chaucer and the Custom of Oral Delivery," *Speculum*, 13 (1938), 413-32; and Mary Elizabeth Giffin, *Studies on Chaucer and His Audience* (Hull, Canada, 1956).

[7] See above, pp. 44-46.

[8] See above, pp. 84-85.

[9] Important biographical works on Caxton are William Blades, *The Life and Typography of William Caxton* (London, 1861-63); Edward Gordon Duff, *William Caxton* (Chicago, 1905); Norman Francis Blake, *Caxton and His World* (London, 1969).

[10] The dates, all approximate, are those given by Blake, *Caxton and His World*, pp. 224-39. The titles are given in the forms used for Chaucer's works by Robinson. Titles of other printed materials associated with Caxton are in the forms given by Seymour de Ricci, *A Census of Caxtons* (Oxford, 1909).

[11] Blake, pp. 34-35.

~§ Chaucer, Published and Printed

¹²The *editio princeps* of Raoul Le Fevre's original work is that printed by the Bruges press *ca.* 1476 (described by de Ricci, *A Census of Caxtons*, pp. 6-7), with which Colard Mansion's name is traditionally associated, although Blake (p. 231) ascribes the printing to Caxton.

¹³Walter John Blyth Crotch, ed., *The Prologues and Epilogues of William Caxton*, EETS, O.S., No. 176 (London, 1928), pp. 4-5. While Crotch's editing is occasionally inaccurate, the volume is convenient, and all references to the prologues and epilogues are to this edition.

¹⁴For further discussion see Crotch, pp. lxxxvi-lxxxviii; and Blake, pp. 55-60.

¹⁵Crotch, p. 7.

¹⁶Described by de Ricci, pp. 3-6.

¹⁷For discussion of Colard Mansion, see Blades, *The Life and Typography of William Caxton*, I, 37-44; Joseph Basile Bernard van Praet, *Notice sur Colard Mansion* (Paris, 1829).

¹⁸Described by de Ricci, passim.

¹⁹The authoritative study of typography as such is that of Daniel Berkeley Updyke, *Printing Types*, 2nd ed. (Cambridge, Mass., 1937). Specimen pages of all of Caxton's types are reproduced on rough paper by de Ricci as a series of frontispieces.

²⁰Geoffrey Ashall Glaister, *An Encyclopedia of the Book* (Cleveland and New York, 1960), pp. 167, 418-19; *Encyclopaedia Britannica*, 14th ed. (Chicago, 1969), XXII, 437-38. See also Joseph Moxon, *Mechanick Exercises in the Whole Art of Printing* (1683-4), ed. Herbert Davis and Harry Carter (London, 1958), pp. 87-133. Moxon's treatise is the first comprehensive manual in any language covering composition, presswork, warehousing, organization, and the service trades of inkmaking, punch cutting, and typefounding. See Philip Gaskell, Giles Barker, and Georgina Warrilow, "An Annotated List of Printers' Manuals to 1850," *Journal of the Printing Historical Society* (No. 4, 1968), 13-14.

²¹For descriptions see Blades, II, xliv-xlvi; *Encyclopaedia Britannica*, XVIII, 547-48; Falconer Madan, "Early Representation of the Printing Press," in *Bibliographica*, ed. Alfred William Pollard, (London, 1895-97), I, 223-48, 499-502. For operation, see Ronald Brunlees McKerrow, *An Introduction to Bibliography for Literary Students* (1928; rpt. Oxford, 1949), pp. 29-37, 57-61; for the carriage, see Michael Pollack, "The Performance of the Wooden Printing Press," *The Library Quarterly*, 42 (1972), 218-64.

²²Blake, pp. 79-81.

[23]Blake, pp. 55-56; 59-60. See also Henry Robert Plomer, *Wynkyn de Worde & His Contemporaries* (London, 1925).

[24]Plomer, pp. 109-53. But see Blake, p. 203.

[25]De Ricci, pp. 3-4.

[26]*Life and Typography*, II, xxxi.

[27]De Ricci, p. 29.

[28]Ibid., pp. 29-30.

[29]Ibid., pp. 46-48.

[30]Ibid., pp. 72-73.

[31]Blake, p. 87; Crotch, p. 37; de Ricci, pp. 11-14.

[32]De Ricci, pp. 18-21.

[33]Crotch, pp. 90-91. In l. 36, Crotch reports "laude" for the "lawde" in the original.

[34]Blake, p. 103.

[35]*The Manuscript Source of Caxton's Second Edition of the Canterbury Tales* (Chicago, 1940).

[36]John Matthews Manly and Edith Rickert, *The Text of the Canterbury Tales* (Chicago, 1940), I, 25, 79-81; II, 57-62. See above, p. 84.

[37]Robinson, pp. xv-xvi.

[38]*The Manuscript Source*, p. 8.

[39]Crotch, p. 69.

[40]Robinson, p. 901.

[41]*The Book of Troilus and Criseyde by Geoffrey Chaucer* (Princeton, 1926), pp. lxi-lxii.

[42]Robinson (p. 905) lists twenty manuscripts, including four which are fragments. A fifth fragment, the Cecil Fragment, has been edited by Jackson Justice Campbell, "A New *Troilus* Fragment," *PMLA*, 73 (1958), 305-08.

[43]Robinson, p. xl.

[44]See above, p. 107.

[45]Blake, pp. 101-24.

[46]De Ricci, pp. 11-14.

[47]Crotch, pp. 20-22; de Ricci, pp. 46-48.

[48]Blake, p. 79.

[49]De Ricci, p. 93.

[50]Alfred William Pollard, *An Essay on Colophons* (Chicago, 1905), p. xviii.

[51]Dard Hunter, *Papermaking*, 2nd ed. (New York, 1957), p. 261. For fuller discussion, see Allan Stevenson, *The Problem of the Missale Speciale* (London, 1967).

[52]See above, p. 120.

[53]De Ricci, p. 9.

[54]See above, p. 53.

[55]De Ricci, p. 53.

[56]Ibid., p. 49.

PLATE XII. Woodcut from Caxton's second edition of the *Canterbury Tales*. (See p. 52 and Plate XI)

Appendix

MONEY AND PRICES

SOME BACKGROUND INFORMATION regarding money is necessary in a study of this kind, for in the period under consideration the entire concept of wages and prices was so different from things as they have been in recent memory that contemporary references such as those examined in the preceding pages have no literal modern equivalents.[1] To talk about medieval prices, as one must surely do in order to discuss books, it is necessary to know something about the currencies involved.

Money in Chaucer's time was very different from, and more valuable than, anything of the sort known now. To begin with, his was a society in which the greater number of people did not have to buy everything they needed. Most lived by agriculture, producing nearly all their own food, as well as housing, furniture, and clothing. The idea that a penny could be a day's wage now seems appalling, but the fact must be seen against an economy in which money played a much smaller role than now in the lives of the common people. In many cases, records show food, clothing, lodging, and other "fringe benefits" given in addition to wages on all levels of society. While people living in towns were more dependent upon cash for their support than were others, by and large the populace had less of it than now and required less, though this has nothing to do with the fundamental instinct to get as much of it as possible!

The currency itself is best understood in terms of its history, which, despite a few necessary incursions into statistics, is a fascinating topic in its own right, especially since some of the coins in question can still be bought, and at prices which are not prohibitive. The most important single fact in the history of English money during the Middle Ages is the gradual adoption, under the Saxon kings, of a silver standard, and the rise to chief importance of the silver denarius traditionally ascribed to Offa the Great, king of Mercia 757-96. The English called their denarius "penny," although they retained *d.* as its symbol. The quality of silver from which English pennies were struck was very high, and the coin achieved and maintained so excellent a reputation that one of the economic problems which plagued the kings in later times was the steady leakage of the coins abroad, where they were hoarded and melted down for silver.

To understand the value of this currency it is necessary to know that it is rated in grains, ounces, and pounds, the grain having been originally a typical one from the middle of an ear of wheat.[2] These terms relate to troy weights, not to the heavier system of avoirdupois. The pound troy now equals 5,700 grains, whereas the pound avoirdupois equals 7,000 gr. But the pound troy under consideration does not precisely fit this description. Instead, it is the mint or tower pound, so called because the London mint was in the Tower of London. The tower pound consisted, until 1529, of 5,400 gr. troy. At the end of Offa's reign the penny, also called for reasons still obscure the "sterling,"[3] weighed 22½ gr., or 240 to the pound tower. The pound of pence or sterlings, with the symbol £ (Lat. *libra* 'pound'), became, and remained the chief English money of account. Likewise a money of account although not itself a coin was the shilling, 12 sterlings or 1/20 of a pound. Less commonly used in domestic transactions was the mark, 160 sterlings or ⅔ of a pound. These moneys of account rest ultimately upon weights, and it is important to know that they were used in other countries, though the weights involved were not everywhere the same.

With their typical genius for making use of existing institutions, the Norman kings continued the penny currency. The names of several generations of Saxon moneyers are evidence that the Conquest brought no sweeping changes to the mint. For a long time the penny was the only coin minted. Small change could be provided by cutting the penny into halves and quarters at the cross on the reverse. Round halfpennies were minted in 1279 and farthings in 1280, the latter well alloyed to produce a size that could be handled.[4]

A great deal of the early money now extant is of course very shabby, due to time, hard wear, and primitive methods of production. Vandalism is another factor, for dishonest persons filed or chipped the edges of coins to obtain silver. Another damaging process was snicking: cutting into the metal to test for genuineness. A cut would reveal the copper core used by counterfeiters. These operations could impair the weight of coins, and hence their negotiability. To discour-

◆§ *Appendix*

age vandalism, the cross on the reverse was elongated, the coin being illegal unless the four ends were visible.[5]

It was up to the individual to see that he was paid in coin of full weight, though the Crown could exercise more power in its own behalf through its sheriffs, who necessarily took care to exact the same from their sources because of ruthless penalties for less than full weight when they brought their tax collections to the tellers of the exchange. In other situations, when a person found himself in possession of money no one would accept because it was too light, he had to have it recoined at the mint at his own expense in order to use it. All these factors are taken as indications that large sums of money were reckoned by weighing, rather than by counting, though it seems likely that the same money was subjected to both processes before it was actually paid.

The mint itself was a very diverse operation in the Middle Ages.[6] In theory, the coin of the realm was issued by the king, and it bore his image. In fact, the image was symbolic, and not at all true portraiture. The kings often did not bother to redesign the coins upon their accession. Some mints, moreover, were episcopal, such as those of York, Durham, and Canterbury, and there was a mint at Bury St. Edmunds. Other mints were scattered about the country, and there were not merely several of them but many, though precisely which were in operation at any given time varied greatly. Any mint consisted of a striking operation and an exchange, which took in material to be coined and distributed the finished money. In Chaucer's time, someone who had silver to sell could either take it to the exchange, which was required to keep a supply of money, and sell it there for cash, or sell directly to the mint, which paid better prices, though he would have to wait about a week for his money to be coined.

The striking operation was done by hammer and die from metal prepared by hand for the purpose. The dies themselves were copied from models which had to be purchased from London. Since dies received a great deal of wear and tear, it was not feasible to reproduce the originals with engraving tools. Instead, the copies were done with punches, a factor responsible for the poor quality of design exhibited by much medieval coin. Another detrimental factor is that the master of the mint often saved himself the cost of making new dies for the reverse of a revised or redesigned coin by using a new die for the obverse (head) but continuing to use the old die for the reverse. Coins thus produced are known to collectors as mules. Moneyers were required to identify their issues by secret marks, which were frequently changed. They were subject to harsh penalties for any abuse of their privileges. Light coin might cost a moneyer his hand.

Since the English had no coin larger than the penny, the increase of trade and of commercial wealth during the thirteenth century throughout Europe put an enormous strain on sterling. International trade was carried out by barter and by gold, which was exchanged chiefly in marks. The mark, like the shilling, was both a weight and a money of account, the English mark being approximately 8 oz., based on the ounce troy, 480 gr. In Europe, the most important gold coins were Italian florins, which had dominated the exchanges since the Florentines produced them in 1282. The design of the original florins showed John the Baptist in full figure, and on the reverse the lily of Florence. They were widely imitated, in Italy and elsewhere. Discrepancies in the weight of the mark from place to place,[7] together with the problem of ascertaining the exact value of gold in relation to silver, meant that even then both merchants and governments were plagued with consequent economic problems, such as balance of trade and hoarding of precious metal abroad.

While the quality of English sterling was excellent, silver was less than satisfactory as a medium of exchange. The process of counting or weighing pence in large sums was cumbersome, and there was a real danger that the sources of silver might become exhausted. Henry III tried to remedy the situation by issuing a gold penny, proclaimed at 20d.[8] But because of problems regarding the relative values of silver and gold the public received the gold penny with so much suspicion that it was eventually discontinued. Edward I had a similar experience when he attempted to issue, between 1279 and 1280, a silver groat, proclaimed at 4d.[9] It was not until the reign of Edward III that either gold coins or silver coins larger than the penny could be successfully introduced.

Besides the awkwardness of reckoning pence in large sums, the English kings had other problems with the currency, not the least being the constant flow of sterling out of the country. In addition, foreign coins of lesser weight, including some made to look like English ones (called *lusshebournes*, or *lussheburghes*, in reference to Luxembourg, where some of them were made), infiltrated in great numbers.

~§ *Appendix*

In 1299, the Statute of Stepney made it illegal (though not impossible) to take coin or precious metal out of the country, or to bring in foreign money, which had to be exchanged at the ports upon entry, a transaction familiar to Chaucer's Merchant, of whom the poet notes ("General Prologue," I, 278), "Wel koude he in eschaunge sheeldes selle." All ports had to elect customs officers to inspect coin, and purchase within the realm was forbidden by any means other than barter or English coins. Smuggling coin was assigned the same penalties as counterfeiting. These measures did not cure the situation, and under Edward III there was a decade when the Crown refused to coin any pence, issuing only halfpence and farthings. Harry Bailly must have had a practiced eye for bogus coins in his business. In the prologue to the Monk's tale, he jokingly compliments that ecclesiast upon his sexuality (VII, 1959-62):

> This maketh that oure wyves wole assaye
> Religious folk, for ye mowe bettre paye
> Of Venus paiementz than mowe we;
> God woot, no lussheburghes payen ye!

Edward finally decided to compete with his neighbors by issuing his own gold coins. A series of English florins, remarkable for their handsome design and fine gold (23 carats, $3\frac{1}{2}$ gr.), which is bright yellow in appearance, was issued in 1343. The name florin was inappropriate, for although the King had hired two Florentine goldsmiths to execute these coins, neither their design nor their value had anything in common with Italian precedent. The English florin, weighing 108 gr., was proclaimed at 6 shillings, double the worth of the Italian florin. Its half and quarter, called from their designs "leopard" and "helm," were valued accordingly.[10] But in this case, as with the gold penny of Henry III, the difficulties of establishing and maintaining a correct ratio between currencies of gold and silver proved disastrous. Edward's advisers had miscalculated in attempting to establish a ratio of about 14 7/9:1 between gold and silver, whereas gold was not at that time worth so much. Now, however, it was impossible to conduct international trade without a gold currency, and a second series was issued, based on an entirely new proportion between gold and silver.

Appendix

These new coins, the noble, its half, and its quarter,[11] started at 80*d*. (6*s*. 8*d*.) for the noble, of 138 6/13 gr. The penny was then devalued to 20¼ gr. At this proportion, 80 pennies weighed 1,620 gr., so that the new ratio of gold to silver was 12½ : 1. There were further adjustments in 1346 and in 1351, bringing the noble down to 120 gr. and the penny to 18 gr., which gave a proportion of 12:1. The currency remained at that proportion during Chaucer's lifetime. The poet therefore knew the following English coins as legal tender: farthing, halfpenny, penny, half groat, groat, quarter noble, half noble, and noble (Plate I). Marks, pounds, and shillings were terms used in accounting, but not English coins.

Excepting Calais, which used English money, the English possessions in France had their own currency, struck on the Continent, often in the style of coins issued by the kings of France. Henry II had issued *deniers* and halves for Aquitaine, but it was under Edward III that Anglo-Gallic coins became artistically interesting. Probably not so much for artistic reasons as to provide himself with a gold currency before he was successful in launching one at home, Edward created handsome gold coins for his French lands: a florin (before 1337), worth 3*s*., designed after its Italian namesake; the *écu* or *chaise d'or* (after 1337), which was soon superseded by the *léopard* of the same value (3*s*. 4*d*.); and the *guiennois* (1360-62), also of the same value. In addition to these, other issues were struck by the Black Prince after 1363. Both Edward and his son also struck sterlings and groats, of course in silver, and a base metal *denier*. The sterling was eventually superseded by another coin called *hardi d'argent*. These issues continued through the reigns of Richard II and Henry IV, notable additions under Henry V being the *mouton d'or*, or *agneau*, showing the *Agnus Dei*, and the *salute*, showing the Annunciation.[12]

Besides the English and Anglo-Gallic coins, Chaucer must have been widely familiar with the moneys of other European countries. As vintners, his family dealt with a product which had to be imported, and in addition to his own experience in the diplomatic service he held the post of Controller of Customs and Subsidy on Wool, Skins, and Hides, in the Port of London. If one were attempting to show what foreign coins such a man must have known, it would be necessary to produce a catalog of European currency. Fortunately, this is not our objective.

Appendix

Coin was in a very dilapidated condition in the second half of the fourteenth century not only in England but on the Continent, due to a shortage of bullion, which the Europeans answered by reducing the size, and hence the value, of their coins. In England the bullion shortage was rendered acute by the foreign wars, and, eventually, by the Wars of the Roses. As foreign trade declined, less precious metal and less foreign coin entered the country for recoining. Toward the close of King Edward's reign, the difficulties of obtaining bullion are evidenced by the fall of the yearly output minted from £2,000 to less than £500, excepting 1374-76, which were good years. Little money was coined under Richard II, whose failure to provide the poor with farthings was one of the grievances that occasioned the Peasants' Revolt of 1381. New coins of his reign are very rare, and money then in circulation was both heavily vandalized and badly worn. In 1411, Henry IV took the radical but necessary measure of issuing new coins with reduced weight while retaining the old currency values. The new noble contained 108 gr. of gold, instead of 120 gr., while the penny dropped to 15 gr. of silver. For approximately twenty years, there was a large coinage on this basis.

Throughout the fifteenth century bullion was scarce, and little coin could be minted. Between 1433 and 1460 less than 7,000 lbs. of gold was minted, an average of only 250 lbs. a year. The coinage of silver was better, but not good. Beginning in 1464, the monetary reforms of Edward IV resorted to the old expedient of devaluing the penny, which was reduced from 15 to 12 gr. The mint was then allowed to purchase silver at an increased price, 33*s.* the pound, instead of the 29*s*, which had been established in 1411. This was achieved by raising the value of the noble from 6*s.* 8*d.* to 8*s.* 4*d.* The king accomplished these measures very swiftly—in fact, within fifteen days—and his success in doing so without fiscal disaster is doubtless due to his replacement of the old noble with a new one, called an "angel," with its half, and to his introduction of a new coin of 10*s.*, called a "ryal" or "rose noble," with its half and quarter.[13] The penny was maintained at 12 gr. The ryal did not survive the Wars of the Roses, and none was struck after 1470 except for special issues under Henry VII, Mary, and Elizabeth. With the accession of Henry VII in 1485 comes a period in which experiments in coin design suggest that year as a point for describing the coinage as no longer medieval. The sovereign, valued at 20*s.*, is the first of the new Tudor coins, and the last coin issued before the change to profile portraiture in which English coins were afterwards designed.[14]

Turning now to the value of the money that has been described, and in this case meaning value in terms of wages and prices, a few statistics will be helpful. The foundation for the study of the cost of living in medieval England is Thorold Rogers' monumental *History of Agriculture and Prices in England.*[15] Much of the information assembled by Rogers pertains, as would be expected, to occupations connected with agriculture as a way of life, and, as he himself suggests, a drawback to the use of these sources is the fact that such records as were kept are likely to be institutional, their prices and amounts being therefore wholesale rather than retail. Nevertheless, the economy of England was at the time indeed primarily agricultural, most of the people deriving their support from farming. Since the supply of food was seasonal it had to be purchased in quantity when available, and, in the absence of modern methods of preservation, kept by such means as were known: cold storage in cellars, salting, pickling, and curing by smoke. A prosperous urban household consisted of servants and apprentices as well as family, and the Paston letters contain enlightening accounts of the work it took for the lady of such an establishment to obtain provisions, and to get them at the best price.[16]

The historical factors that conditioned wages and prices in Chaucer's time and in the century following are well known. At the beginning of the fourteenth century, there was a period of some twenty years when harvests were poor and when food was both scarce and expensive. Afterwards, the spoils of the French wars, together with a rapid increase of trade, brought commercial prosperity. Prices and wages were increasing briskly when in 1348-49 the Black Death struck, carrying off a large portion of the population, and producing a serious labor shortage. Wages increased as much as 150%, and many villeins used the labor shortage to bargain for their freedom. The movement was at least discouraged in 1351 by the Statute of Laborers, a largely unsuccessful attempt at a wage freeze which festered in the minds of the peasants until the revolt of 1381 in the reign of Richard II.[17] By the beginning of the fifteenth century, however, villeinage had all but disappeared, the former serf having become a rent-paying tenant, free from the worst of feudal obligations, forced labor. The rise in prices and wages brought about by the Plague con-

Appendix

tinued until about 1370, wages thereafter remaining fairly stable until the beginning of the sixteenth century, despite the disastrous wars in France and civil wars at home.

It is simpler to discuss wages than to discuss prices, which involve quantities weighed, counted, or measured by standards now frequently obsolete, obscure, or sufficiently different from those of modern times to be extremely confusing. And, since the available records show prices which are for the most part wholesale, it is impossible to make valid generalizations about small purchases, a matter complicated by the fact that so many of the necessities of life were not purchased but made in the home by much of the population. Wages, on the other hand, represent specific services performed for a fee. The actual cash wages, of course, can have little meaning until prices, too, are considered, the important thing being what one's money will buy at a point in time. But here also the available statistics do not reveal information that later times would like to know, such as how many days in a particular year someone actually worked and earned the going daily wage. The reasoning behind a particular wage, moreover, is not always apparent, such matters as custom, age, and experience being factors that do not necessarily show in the records. Other factors that might enter into a wage without showing in records of cash transactions would include gifts of clothing, food, and lodging. Wages, too, might be higher in different places for the same service, and wages for various types of seasonal and urgent work connected with the harvest, such as reaping, might be high but of short duration. It must be remembered throughout these comments on wages and prices that the money actually paid is based on the penny: shillings did not exist as coins. With these comments in mind, it will be useful to list some representative wages, using Rogers' statistics, and giving them in the averages (per diem, unless stated otherwise) he computes by decades rather than giving them, as he also does, year by year:

Appendix

	Thatcher	Helper	Reaper Wheat (acre)	Thresher Wheat(East) (quarter)	Carpenter	Mason
	d.	d.	d.	d.	d.	d.
1341-50	2 ⅞	1 ⅛	6 ⅛	3 ⅜	3 ⅛	3 ½
1351-60	3 ½	2	7 ¾	3 ¼	4 ¼	4 ⅞
1361-70	3 ½	2	7 ⅛	4 ¾	4 ¼	5 ⅜
1371-80	4 ⅛	2 ½	10	5	5	6 ⅛
1381-90	3 ⅞	2 ⅛	10	3 ½	4 ¾	6
1391-1400	4 ⅛	2 ⅝	7 ⅜	...	4 ⅝	5 ⅝
1401-10	4 ½	3	7	3 ¾	5 ½	6
1411-20	4 ¾	3	7 ¼	3 ¾	5 ¼	6
1421-30	4 ½	3	8	3 ¾	5 ½	5 ½
1431-40	4 ½	3 ¼	12 ½	4 ½	6	6
1441-50	5 ¼	4	11 ½	4 ⅝	5 ¾	6 ¼
1451-60	5 ½	3 ¼	10 ½	4 ¼	6	6 ¼
1461-70	4 ¾	3 ¾	10	3 ¾	6	6 ¼
1471-80	5 ¼	3 ¾	....	2 ¾	5 ¾	6 ¼
1481-90	6	3 ¾	....	3	6	5 ¾
1491-1500	5 ½	3 ½	....	4 ¼	6	5 ¾ [18]

The fact that these statistics are averages produces fractions that do not represent cash actually paid; dots indicate that figures are lacking.

These representative wages become more meaningful when compared with representative prices. Prices, as noted earlier, are not so easy to present, because of problems in interpreting the weights, measures, and counts by which goods were sold. The English system of weights and measures was originally based on the weight of 32 grains of average wheat taken from the middle of the ear at the time of harvest.[19] This weight amounts to approximately 22 ½ gr. troy, the original weight of the penny (pennyweight, dwt.). Pennies to the number of 240 equalled the tower pound, 5,400 gr., which was the pound sterling. Whether the tower pound, rather than the pound troy (5,700 gr.), was the standard pound for all weights and measures is another question. There is, moreover, evidence of another pound used in merchandise transactions: one of 15 oz. Indeed, there were often several, if not many, local and trade variations of particular weights and measures. Within these terms, and in dry measure, the gallon was 8 lbs., the bushel 8 gals., the quarter 8 bu. Of all the

Appendix

common measures, however, the petra (stone) is the most difficult to understand. There are records of petrae of 5 lbs., 7, 8, 9, 12, 13, 14, 15, 16, 17, 18, 19, 20, and 21 lbs., most of these pertaining to wool. The petra for weighing animals, including humans, was 14 lbs. One of 8 lbs. was employed in measuring the hundred of 13½ petrae used in the purchase and sale of wax, sugar, pepper, almonds, and cumin. But there were also many hundreds. An ancient one equalled 108 lbs. That generally used by London merchants equaled 112 lbs.

Much of the application of this or that weight or measure to particular commodities is a matter of custom, the origins being lost in tradition. The pondus, pisa, or wey was used for wool, for cheese, and sometimes for butter. Cheese was also measured by the clove (7 lbs.), and a wey of cheese was supposed to contain 32 cloves of 7 lbs., but there are records of cloves of 6½ and 8 lbs. These particular weights are avoirdupois, the pound avoir. consisting of 7,000 gr.

There were, of course, other measures besides those by weight. Linear measures for textiles were the ell (for linen), and the yard, for all other fabric, though textiles other than linen were usually sold by the piece or panus (24 yards). Other measures were by count or tale, again governed largely by custom. Examples are the hundred (not to be confused with the weight of the same name), which might be more than 100, as, for example, the hundred of 120 for eggs, nails, and cheaper fish; the barrel or thousand, which was supposed to be ten times larger than the hundred, whatever it was, as 1200 for herring; the last, which was, for herring, 12 barrels; the dozen, chiefly for game and the rarer kinds of fish. Liquid measures were the gill, usually ¼ pint; the pint, 4 gills; the quart, 2 pints; the pottle, 2 quarts; the gallon, 4 quarts. Other liquid measures were the tun, generally 252 gallons; the pipe, 126 gallons; and the sextary, 4-6 gallons. These last instances pertain to wine or cider.

The commodities here listed by price are selected for a variety of reasons to represent prices typical of the cost of living, not the least important reason being that the statistics are available and understandable without complex prefatory discussion. The reader may wonder why those mainstays of the diet, bread and ale, are missing. While scattered statistics are available, these products tended to be made in the home, so that the best records are the prices of wheat and barley. As noted earlier, the prices are gathered from institutional records, so that the averages listed are wholesale, not retail, though

Appendix

there is good reason to believe that much purchase, even for provisioning private households, was indeed by large amounts.

I. Dairy Products

	Cheese pisa (wey)		Butter gal.		Eggs hund. (120)
	s.	d.	s.	d.	d.
1341-50	8	4	0	8¼	4⅜
1351-60	10	9¼	0	8¾	5
1361-70	10	2½	0	9	4¾
1371-80	9	5¾	0	9¼	5¼
1381-90	9	6	0	6½	5
1391-1400	10	2	0	8	5¼
1401-10	10	6½	0	8	5⅛
1411-20	10	8	1	0	4¼
1421-30	10	2½	0	8	4¾
1431-40	..	...	.	...	5¾
1441-50	..	...	0	11½	5¾
1451-60	..	...	0	11¾	5½
1461-70	6	11	0	7	5
1471-80	6	6	0	9½	5½
1481-90	..	...	0	11½	5¼
1491-1500	7	11½	0	10½	5½[20]

Cheese was commonly formed in three sizes: small, medium, and large, which usually sold retail at 1*d.*, 2*d.*, and 3*d.*, and which weighed, Rogers believes, 2 lbs., 4 lbs., and 6 lbs. Milk was sold at 1*d.* per gal. in the second half of the fourteenth century, rising to 3*d.* in the fifteenth. Butter had more uses than as food, being a lubricating agent and also the principal ingredient, mixed with tar, in the only effective cure for sheep scab then known. Its price fluctuates more than the price of cheese.

·§ *Appendix*

II. Meat, Poultry, and Fish

	Porci (presumably hogs ready for butchering)		*Capons*	*Herring m=1200*	
	s.	d.	d.	s.	d.
1341-50	2	8½	2¾	9	3
1351-60	3	1¾	3⅝	13	8½
1361-70	3	8	4	13	4
1371-80	3	2¼	3⅞	14	4¾
1381-90	3	3	3½	15	3¼
1391-1400	3	2	3½	18	2¾ [21]

	Hogs (highest prices)		*Capons*	*Herring Red (cade)*		*White (barrel)*	
	s.	d.	d.	s.	d.	s.	d.
1401-10	1	10½	4	6	2¼	11	2
1411-20	1	6½	4	7	5½	16	0
1421-30	1	6¾	4	6	6½	13	7
1431-40	1	8	4	7	11	10	8¼
1441-50	1	4¾	4	6	2¾	10	0
1451-60	1	0¾	4	6	9	10	11½
1461-70	1	5¾	4	7	1	9	10½
1471-80	1	6	4½	6	6½	12	0
1481-90	1	4½	5	4	11¼	10	9¾
1491-1500	.	...	6¾	4	9	9	11 [22]

Appendix

III. Grain (quarter)

	Wheat		Barley		Peas	
	s.	d.	s.	d.	s.	d.
1341-50	5	3⅛	3	8½	2	11⅜
1351-60	6	10⅝	4	7	3	11¼
1361-70	7	3¼	5	0⅛	4	4⅝
1371-80	6	1¼	3	10¼	3	3¼
1381-90	5	2	3	4⅜	3	4¼
1391-1400	5	3	3	5⅞	3	5
1401-10	5	8¼	3	11¾	3	3¼
1411-20	5	6¾	3	8½	3	3¾
1421-30	5	4¾	3	7	3	2¼
1431-40	6	11	3	10	3	8
1441-50	5	3¾	2	11	2	8¼
1451-60	5	6½	3	2¼	2	10
1461-70	5	4½	3	3½	2	11
1471-80	5	4¼	3	3½	3	5¼
1481-90	6	3½	4	5¾	4	2¼
1491-1500	5	0¾	3	6¼	3	7¼ [23]

IV. Textiles

	Table Linen doz. ells.		Canvas doz. ells.	
	s.	d.	s.	d.
1341-50	3	0¼	2	5½
1351-60	5	3½	6	5
1361-70	6	8	5	3¼
1371-80	7	6	5	1½
1381-90	7	2	3	9¼
1391-1400	6	4¼	3	9½
1401-10	6	8½	4	6
1411-20	6	2½	4	7½
1421-30	6	5	5	0¼
1431-40	5	9¾	4	8½
1441-50	7	0¾	3	3
1451-60	5	0½	4	3
1461-70	6	2½	4	2
1471-80	7	4	5	0
1481-90	7	4¼	4	0
1491-1500	7	6¾	4	3¾ [24]

Appendix

V. Miscellaneous

	Candles doz. lbs.		Wine doz. gals.	
	s.	d.	s.	d.
1341-50	1	9¾	10	1½
1351-60	2	0¾	8	1
1361-70	2	2½	8	11¼
1371-80	2	0½	9	6
1381-90	1	9½	7	11¼
1391-1400	1	7¼	6	6½
1401-10	1	6¾	7	8½ (red)
1411-20	1	5½	6	5
1421-30	1	6½	7	2¼
1431-40	1	6¼	7	0¼
1441-50	1	4½	8	0
1451-60	1	3	7	8
1461-70	1	3¾	8	9
1471-80	1	2	8	3½
1481-90	1	3	9	4½
1491-1500	1	0½	8	10¾ [25]

It is interesting to note from these statistics that wages increased faster than prices during the period 1341-1500. Had it not been for the wars of the time, and for such domestic blunders as the Statute of Laborers (1351), the English worker would have been better off in Chaucer's time than before the Black Death.

It would, of course, be possible to compile a longer list of wages and prices, or even a different list, but this has seemed adequate for present purposes. Economists would doubtless prefer to use indexes instead of prices, but in a study primarily intended for literary interests this presents too many preliminary problems and does not lend itself to particular cases. The information here presented should give meaning and perspective to all remarks of an economic nature that have been made in this volume pertaining to the milieu of books known to Chaucer and to those who published his works, both in manuscript and in the earliest endeavors of the printing press.

Appendix

NOTES TO APPENDIX

[1] For a brief introduction to the subject of wages and prices, see John Burnett, *A History of the Cost of Living* (Harmondsworth, Eng., 1969), pp. 9-54.

[2] For these and other weights and measures, see Ronald Edward Zupko, *A Dictionary of English Weights and Measures* (Madison, Wisc., 1968). Zupko does not discuss coins or moneys of account, except indirectly.

[3] Various theories are summarized by the *Oxford English Dictionary* (Oxford, 1933), X, 927-28. For photographs of Offa's penny, see George Cyril Brooke, *English Coins*, 3rd ed., rev. (London, 1950), Plate V, nos. 2-20.

[4] Brooke, *English Coins*, Plate XXIV, nos. 1-11.

[5] Cf. Brooke, Plate XXII, nos. 1, 11.

[6] John Craig, *The Mint* (Cambridge, 1953).

[7] For lists of medieval values throughout Europe, see Charles Du Fresne Du Cange, *Glossarium ad Scriptores Mediae et Infimae Latinitatis* (Paris, 1840-50), IV, 271-72. All moneys, past and present, are defined, in terms of their gold or silver content and fineness, in Franz Pick and René Sédillot, *All the Monies of the World* (New York, 1971).

[8] Brooke, Plate XXII, no. 25.

[9] Brooke, Plate XXIII, no. 1.

[10] Reginald Hugh Dolley, "Coinage," in *Medieval England*, ed. Austin Lane Poole, rev. ed. (Oxford, 1958), I, Plate 34, *b, c, d*.

[11] Dolley, Plate 34, *e, f, g*.

[12] Dolley, Plate 33.

[13] Dolley, Plate 35, *b, c*.

[14] Dolley, Plate 35, *d*.

[15] (Oxford, 1866-1902).

[16] James Gairdner, ed. *The Paston Letters, A.D. 1422-1509* (London, 1904), II, 229, 267, 276-77; III, 283; IV, 14.

[17] For short, authoritative discussions, see George Macaulay Trevelyan, *History of England*, new ed. (London, New York, and Toronto, 1937), pp. 236-50; A. R. Myers, *England in the Late Middle Ages*, rev. ed. (Harmondsworth, Eng., 1963). A useful popular discussion is Philip Lindsay and Reg Groves, *The Peasants' Revolt, 1381* (New York, 1950).

~§ Appendix

[18]Rogers, *Agriculture and Prices*, I, 320-22; IV, 524-25. Statistics before 1401 are based on the highest prices paid. For threshing, Rogers gives regional statistics, from which those from the east are here reported (Lincolnshire, Norfolk, Suffolk, Essex, and Kent). He lists separately highest and average wages paid for carpenters after 1400. The average wage has been quoted here. The rest of the statistics represent average wages.

[19]For further discussion, see Rogers, I, 164-72.

[20]Rogers, I, 452; IV, 381. Rogers gives some of these statistics in decimals, here converted to fractions.

[21]Rogers, I, 362-63, 641.

[22]Rogers, IV, 355-56, 545. The statistics are here presented separately from those of the fourteenth century because Rogers' sources give different breakdowns of the items involved. A cade is a barrel of 720 herring.

[23]Rogers, I, 245; IV, 292.

[24]Rogers, I, 593; IV, 589.

[25]Rogers, I, 453, 641; IV, 381, 690.

Selected Bibliography

Adamson, J. W. "The Extent of Literacy in England in the Fifteenth and Sixteenth Centuries: Notes and Conjectures." *The Library*, 4th Ser., 10 (1929-30), 163-93.

Bell, H. E. "The Price of Books in Medieval England." *The Library*, 4th Ser., 17 (1937), 312-32.

Bennett, Henry Stanley. "The Author and His Public in the Fourteenth and Fifteenth Centuries." *Essays and Studies by Members of the English Association*, 23 (1938), 7-24.

Blades, William. *The Life and Typography of William Caxton, England's First Printer*, 2 vols. London: Lilly, 1861, 1863.

Blake, Norman Francis. *Caxton and His World*. London: Deutsch, 1969.

Brooke, George Cyril. *English Coins from the Seventh Century to the Present Day*. 3rd ed., rev. London: Methuen, 1950.

Bühler, Curt Ferdinand. *The Fifteenth-Century Book: The Scribes, the Printers, the Decorators*. Philadelphia: Univ. of Pennsylvania Press, 1960.

Cappelli, Adriano. *Dizionario di abbreviature latine ed italiane*. Milan: Hoepli, 1929.

Clark, John Willis. *The Care of Books: An Essay on the Development of Libraries and their Fittings, from the Earliest Times to the End of the Eighteenth Century*. 2nd ed. Cambridge: The University Press, 1909.

Crotch, Walter John Blyth, ed. *The Prologues and Epilogues of William Caxton*. EETS, O.S., No. 176. London: Milford, 1928.

Destrez, Jean. *La Pecia dans les manuscrits universitaires du XIIIe et du XIVe siècle*. Paris: Vautrain, 1935.

Diringer, David. *The Illuminated Book: Its History and Production*. Rev. ed. New York: Praeger, 1967.

Bibliography

The Ellesmere Chaucer Reproduced in Facsimile. 2 vols. Manchester: The University Press, 1911.

Galbraith, Vivian Hunter. "Handwriting." In *Medieval England,* ed. Austin Lane Poole, 2 vols., new ed., rev. Oxford: Clarendon Press, 1958. II, 541-58.

Goldschmidt, Ernst Philipp. *Gothic & Renaissance Bookbindings.* 2 vols. London: Benn, 1928.

Hind, Arthur Mayger. *An Introduction to a Study of Woodcut.* 2 vols. Boston: Houghton Mifflin, 1935.

Hobson, Geoffrey Dudley. *English Binding Before 1500.* Cambridge: The University Press, 1929.

Hunter, Dard. *Papermaking: The History and Technique of an Ancient Craft.* 2nd ed., rev. New York: Knopf, 1957.

Lowe, Elias Avery. "Handwriting." In Crump, Charles George, and Ernest Fraser Jacob, eds. *The Legacy of the Middle Ages.* Oxford: Clarendon Press, 1943. Pp. 197-226.

McKerrow, Ronald Brunlees. *An Introduction to Bibliography for Literary Students.* 1928; rpt. Oxford: Clarendon Press, 1949.

Manly, John Matthews, and Edith Rickert. *The Text of the Canterbury Tales: Studied on the Basis of All Known Manuscripts.* 8 vols. Chicago: Univ. of Chicago Press, 1940.

Millar, Eric George. *English Illuminated Manuscripts from the Xth to the XIIIth Century.* Paris: Van Oest, 1926.

_____. *English Illuminated Manuscripts of the XIVth and XVth Centuries.* Paris: Van Oest, 1928.

Muscatine, Charles. *The Book of Geoffrey Chaucer.* San Francisco: The Book Club of California, 1963.

Panofsky, Erwin. *Early Netherlandish Painting: Its Origins and Character.* 2 vols. Cambridge, Mass.: Harvard Univ. Press, 1953.

Parkes, Malcolm Beckwith. *English Cursive Book Hands 1250-1500.* Oxford: Clarendon Press, 1969.

Pollard, Graham. "The Construction of English Twelfth-Century Bindings." *The Library,* 5th Ser., 17 (1962), 1-22.

Bibliography

───────. "The Names of Some English Fifteenth-Century Binders." *The Library*, 5th Ser., 25(1970), 193-218.

Ricci, Seymour de. *A Census of Caxtons*. Bibliographical Society, London, Illustrated Monograph No. 15. Oxford: The University Press, 1909.

Rickert, Margaret. "Illumination." In Manly and Rickert, *The Text of the Canterbury Tales*, I, 561-605.

───────. *Painting in Britain: The Middle Ages*. London: Penguin, 1954.

Robinson, Fred Norris, ed. *The Works of Geoffrey Chaucer*. 2nd ed. Boston: Houghton Mifflin, 1957.

Rogers, James E. Thorold. *A History of Agriculture and Prices in England*. 7 vols. in 8. Oxford: Clarendon Press, 1866-1902.

Root, Robert Kilburn. "Publication before Printing." *PMLA*, 28 (1913), 417-31.

Spielmann, Marion Harry. *The Portraits of Geoffrey Chaucer*. Chaucer Society, 2nd Ser., No. 31. London: Trübner, 1900.

Thompson, Edward Maunde. *An Introduction to Greek and Latin Palaeography*. Oxford: Clarendon Press, 1912.

Wattenbach, Wilhelm. *Das Schriftwesen im Mittelalter*. 3rd ed. Leipzig: Hirzel, 1896.

Weiss, Roberto. *Humanism in England During the Fifteenth Century*. Medium Aevum Monographs, No. 4. Oxford: Blackwell, 1941.

Zupko, Ronald Edward. *A Dictionary of English Weights and Measures from Anglo-Saxon Times to the Nineteenth Century*. Madison, Wisc.: Univ. of Wisconsin Press, 1968.

Index

Adam, Chaucer's scribe, 58-59, 65, 84, 89, 95, 96
Anelida and Arcite, 94, 116, 123
Anglicana book hands. *See* Paleography
Angoulême, John of, 79-80
Anne of Bohemia, 36, 46, Plate VI

Beccaria, Antonio, 107
Benedict, Saint, 59, 101
Bestiaries, 30
Bibliothèque Nationale (Paris) manuscript: Fonds Anglais, 39, 79-80
Bibliothèque Royale de Belgique (Brussels) manuscript: Bib. Roy. 4862-4864, 37
Black Death, 33, 147, 154
Boccaccio, Giovanni, 105, 114
Bodmer Library (Geneva) manuscript: Phillipps 8136, 21
Boece, 65, 84, 93, 94, 115, 116, 124-25, 133
Book of the Duchess, 115
Book trade: liturgical books, 31, 96-98; part of Chaucer's milieu, 89, 92-93, 100-05; secular books, 90, 93, 118; academic books, 98-99
Bookbinding: significance for Chaucer scholars, 3-5; finish of, 4, 15, 16-21; closing devices, 4, 16-17, 21; process of, 15-21; ornament in, 18, 21, 23, 24; economics of, 24, 25; Plates II, III
Bracciolini, Poggio, 106
Brailes, W. de, 37
British Museum, manuscripts: Add. 5140, 13, 49; Add. 10340, 18; Add. 16165, 94; Egerton 2863, 48; Harley 1758, 40, 49; Harley 4334, 48; Harley 4866, 38, 43-44; Harley 7334, 78; Lansdowne 851, 46, 48; Royal 17.D.vi, 38, 43
Bruges, Louis de, 119
Bury, Richard de, 100, 104, 107, 114

Cambridge University, manuscripts: Gg.4.27, 39-41, 78-79, 84; Mm. 2.5, 48; Corpus Christi College, manuscript, 61, 38, 44, 46, Plate VI; Peterhouse, manuscripts, 114 and 154, 25; Trinity College, manuscripts: R.3.3, 49, R.3.20, 94, R.14, 5-6, 45
Canterbury Tales: portraits of pilgrims, 30, 38, 39-40, 41; Caxton's first edition, 52, 116, 126-29; Caxton's second edition, 52, 53, 117, 125-30, 133, 134, 135-36; Pynson's edition, 53, 135; Wynkyn de Worde's edition, 53, 135; editorial problems, 77, 82, 84-85, 128-29
—references to pilgrims: Clerk, 3, 18, 25, 91, 92; Franklin, 83; Knight, 79, 80, 81-82; Man of Law, 78-79, 85; Merchant, 144; Monk, 105, 144; Parson, 40, 41, 78; Physician, 78; Second Nun, 78; "Sir Thopas," 93; Wife of Bath, 81, 83, 115-16
Caxton, William: paper of, 7, 10, 11-12, 13-14; as editor, 14, 52, 81, 84, 116-17, 123, 124, 125-33, 135-36; binder of, 24; life of, 24, 100, 117-19, 124, 135; woodcuts of, 52, 53, 134-35, Plate XII; typography of, 76, 120-21, 123, 133-34, Plates X, XI; press at Westminster, 100, 122-24, 133; press at Bruges, 118-20, 125, 131; books compared to other incunabula, 134
Cennini, Cennino, 29
Charles V, king of France, 109
Charles, duke of Burgundy, 118, 122
Chaucer, Geoffrey: 106, 145, 147, 154; and milieu of books, 3, 5, 17, 21, 25, 30, 89, 92-93, 100, 103, 104-05; and milieu of art, 29, 30, 32, 33, 36-37, 54; portraits of, 29, 38, 39, 41-46, 54; as writer, 29, 82-83, 84, 113-16; persona of, 44, 89, 109; and scribe Adam, 58-59, 65, 89, 95, 96; short poems, 58, 86, 115-16, 123. *See also* titles of major works
Chaucer, Thomas, 95

Delamere, MS., 48
Devonshire, MS., 38, 46, 49

163

Index 🙰

Dickens, Charles, 30
Duccio, painter, 33
Dürer, Albrecht, 50, 52, 53
Duxworth, John, 79-80

Editing, 77-85, 116, 125-33
Edward III, 144, 145
Edward IV, 108, 118, 119, 122, 146
Ellesmere, MS.: art of, 29-30, 38-39, 48, 50, 54, 100; portrait of Chaucer, 38-39, 41, 43, 44, 46, Plate V; authority of, 80, 84; textual problems in, 80-81, 128-29, 135-36

Frulovisi, Tito Livio, 107

Gatherings (quires): 5, 12; materials of (parchment and vellum), 5-6, 7, 10-12, 16; materials of (paper), 7, 10, 11-12, 13, 24, 134; folding of, 12-13, 14; foliation, 14-15; signatures, 14-15, 134
Gaunt, John of, 115
Gothic script. *See* Paleography
Gower, John, 40
Guarino da Verona, 107
Gutenberg, John, 7, 51

Hengwrt, MS. *See* National Library of Wales
Henry II, 145
Henry III, 143, 144
Henry IV, 106-07, 123, 145, 146
Henry V, 106, 145
Henry VI, 106, 107
Herman, Richard, 44
Hoccleve, Thomas, 43, 44, 46, 54
House of Fame, 109, 117, 130-31
Humanism, 93, 94, 106, 107
Humphrey, duke of Gloucester, 106-07
Huntington Library, manuscripts: Ellesmere, *See* entry; HM 144, 19, Plate II; HM 195, 51; HM 26052, 17

Illumination: initials, 15, 28, 30, 31, 46, 47, 134; miniatures, 28-29, 31, 32-33, 36, 45-46, 50; International style, 29-30, 33, 36, 44, 46, 50, Plate VI; Romanesque art, 30, 31, 32; Gothic art, 31-32; East Anglian style, 32-33, 37, 48; portraiture, 38-46, 50; illumination in Chaucer MSS, 47-50
Incipits, 21

Incunabula, 50, 52, 76, 134
Ink, 51-52, 122

James I, king of Scotland, 11

Kells, Book of, 61

Le Fevre, Raoul, 118, 119, 120, 124
Legend of Good Women, 82, 89
Lettou, John, 133
Libraries: facilities of, 89, 101, 103-04; private, 93-94, 104-09; lending, 96, 101-02; monastic, 101, 102-03; university, 103-04
Lichfield Cathedral, MS. 2, 48
Limbourg brothers, 33
Lindisfarne Gospels, 61
Longleat 257, MS., 49
Lovell, John, Lord, 37
Lyttington Missal. *See* Westminster Abbey

Machinia, William de, 134
Mansion, Colard, 119-20, 122
Margaret of York, 118, 122
Mercers, 100
Merchants Adventurers, 117, 123
Monasticism, 59, 90, 113
Money: 21, 23, 140-47; Italian, 11-12, 143; French, 11, 92; English, 140-47; Anglo-Gallic, 145
Montefeltro, Federico da, 4
Morgan Library (New York City), manuscripts: Campsall, 107, 132, Plate IX; Windmill Psalter, 32, 33, Plate IV

National Library of Scotland (Edinburgh), manuscript, Auchinleck, 93
National Library of Wales (Aberystwyth), manuscript, Hengwrt, 78, 82, 84
Norman Conquest, 30, 37

Orléans, Charles d', 79-80
Oxford Fragments, 40, 49
Oxford University: Merton College, accounts of, 10, 11; humanism at, 107; Corpus Christi College, 48, 198
—manuscripts: Bodley 686, 38, 46, 49; Hatton Donat 1, 49; Laud 600, 49; Rawlinson Poetry 223, 46-49; Selden Arch. B.14, 23, 49, Plate III

164

Index

Paleography: 59; majuscules, 60-61; cursives, 60-61, 65-66; alphabet, 60, 62-63; minuscules, 61-63; abbreviation, 63-65, 80-81; Gothic script, 63-65, 66, 77, 91, 133; duct, 65, 66; Secretary book hands, 65, 67, 76-77, 123, Plate VIII; Anglicana book hands, 65-67, 76-77, Plates VII, IX
Paper. *See* Gatherings
Parchment. *See* Gatherings
Paris, Matthew, 37
Parliament of Fowls, 115, 116, 124
Paston family, 11, 108, 147
Patronage, 113, 114, 124
Peasants' Revolt, 113, 146, 147
Pecia, 90-92, 98, 103
Petrarch, Francesco, 105, 114
Petworth, MS., 48
Phillipps 8250, MS., 132
Pratt, William, 124-25
Prices, representative, 151-54
Prince, Gilbert, 44
Printing: earliest, 50-51; Vespasiano da Bisticci on, 94; prices of printed books, 100-01; forms, 120, 121-22; earliest presses, 121-22. *See also* Woodcut, Incunabula, Caxton
Publication, 90, 113-14, 115
Pucelle, Jean, 32, 98
Pynson, Richard, 24, 52, 53, 123, 135

Ravenstone, William de, 105
Richard II, 36, 44, 46, 99, 113, 146, 147, Plate VI
Ripoli Press (Florence), 11-12
Roman de la Rose, 93, 96, 99, 100
Rood, Theodore, 133

Saint Paul's Cathedral, manuscript, A 67/46, 105, 112, *n*51

Scheere, Herman, 37-38
Scribes, 12, 58-60, 65, 76, 77-83, 85-86, 95
Scriptorium, 59-60, 90, 93
Secretary book hands. *See* Paleography
Shakespeare, William, 30
Shirley, John, 94-95, 116
Siferwas, John, 37-38
Stationers: university, 90-92; urban, 93-95, 116
Statute of Laborers, 147, 154
Statute of Stepney, 144
Sutra, Diamond, 50-51

Tate, John, 10
Tiptoft, John, earl of Worcester, 107-08
Title pages, 21, 134
Tolleshurst, William de, 105
Treatise on Astrolabe, 37

Universities, 59, 90-92, 96, 103-04

Van der Weyden, Roger, 33
Van Eyck, Jan, 33
Variant readings, 77-85
Vellum. *See* Gatherings
Vespasiano da Bisticci, 4, 93-94, 95, 108
Visconti library (Milan), 104-05

Wages, representative, 148-49
Wars of the Roses, 107, 118, 146
Weights and measures, 10, 11, 141, 149-50
Westminster Abbey, manuscripts: *Liber Regalis*, 36; Lytlington Missal, 24, 95, 97
Woodcut, 24, 28, 47, 50-53, 134
Worde, Wynkyn de, 10, 21, 24, 52, 53, 123, 134, 135